Selections from ~ ~ ~

The
Joy
of
Eating

A Simply Delicious Cookbook
by Renny Darling

Compliments of

CALIFORNIA FEDERAL

S0-DVG-563

ACKNOWLEDGMENTS

My warmest thanks to Milli Levin, artist and old friend for all her help in decorating and illustrating the pages of this book . . . But above all for her interest and her caring. I owe a debt of gratitude to Sharron Polkinghorne, caligrapher and new friend for her wonderful effort and her interest above and beyond the call of friendship. I want to thank my dear friends Carol Greenfield, Sheila Howard and Carol Provisor for being the inspiration for so many of these dishes throughout the years. Their constant raves and support encouraged me to create bigger and better dishes for our Wednesday afternoon luncheons.

My deepest thanks to my wonderful family for their help and support and encouragement and for eating mousses seven days in a row until I arrived at the simplicity I was looking for. Believe it, eating mousses can also be a labor of love. My thanks to my mother-in-law who shared many of her favorite recipes and to my mother who is an extraordinary cook and baker and who instilled in me a love for delicious food and *THE JOY OF EATING*.

First Printing	*September, 1976*
Second Printing	*November, 1976*
Third Printing	*February, 1977*
Fourth Printing	*April, 1977*
Fifth Printing	*May, 1977*
Sixth Printing	*June, 1977*
Seventh Printing	*December, 1977*
Eighth Printing	
Special Edition	*December, 1977*
Ninth Printing	*January, 1978*

Published by Recipes-of-the-Month Club
P.O. Box 5027, Beverly Hills, California 90210
Printed in the United States of America
Library of Congress Catalog Card Number: 76-27499
ISBN 0-930440-07-2

The Introduction

I must confess that I do not like to chore in the kitchen one bit more than necessary. Chopping onions does absolutely nothing for me except make me cry. However, I do love and adore delicious food, prepared in an exciting and different manner. *THE JOY OF EATING* originated out of these two notions ... the desire for exquisite tasting dishes, prepared in the minimum amount of time.

This book is dedicated to the preparation of delectable dishes with minimum technique. A blender or a mixer does most of the work for you. The main emphasis is taste ... rich, glorious and pleasurable ... with recipes that promise to get you out of the kitchen in a hurry.

As an example, my recipe for Cherry Glazed Chicken Breasts Stuffed with Wild Rice can be made quite differently. You can start with fresh cherries, scrub them, stem them, seed them .. cook them with sugar ... you can squeeze the oranges and strain the juice ... then you can thicken the glaze with corn starch ... and so on. Results might be slightly better exerting all this effort. And it's great ... if you happen to have the time.

However, if you do not, using the black cherry preserves, frozen orange juice and a delightful liqueur takes seconds to assemble and the results are also marvellously delicious.

The recipes in this book minimize last minute preparation. If you are cooking for your family or your friends, you owe them the pleasure of your company. But, also, you owe yourself the luxury and the enjoyment of being a guest at your own party. Most of the dishes can be assembled or cooked earlier in the day, leaving the simple task of reheating at time of serving.

3

I hope you own several of the lovely porcelain servers that are also so good for baking and storing. For me, they are indispensable.

Lastly, a dish should delight in its TASTE and should not promise more than it can deliver. Did you ever see a pastry cart, laden with the most delectable looking pastries? Then comes the agony of decision. What to choose? . . . the chocolate petit four, the raspberry roll, the eclair with the rosettes on top? Then one bite and the music goes out of the day. You feel let down. The TASTE never delivered what it promised. So, while you garnish, embellish and decorate to your heart's content, keep in mind, it's the pleasure of the taste that delivers *THE JOY OF EATING.*

A few last words before you begin . . .

— Always read a recipe over very carefully. Then assemble all your ingredients before you start the preparation.

— Always preheat your oven.

— The amounts of salt to use have been left to your personal preference.

— COOKING TIMES are always approximate due to slight variations in oven temperatures, the kind of pan you are using, etc. Look for the description in the recipe to guide you, such as . . . "until a cake tester inserted in center comes out clean," or until top is lightly browned", etc.

— The number of people served is also approximate, depending on the number of courses and the size of the portions you are serving, etc.

— ORANGE ZEST is the essence of the orange flavor and is obtained by grating the outer skin of the orange. It does not include the white part (the pith) as does Orange Peel.

The Contents

THE CONTENTS (Cont.)

THE CONTENTS (Cont.)

THE CONTENTS (Cont.)

THE CONTENTS (Cont.)

DESSERTS (Cont.)

For Harry, Joey, Jeffy & Debby
who are the Joys of my life—
and who I love
very, very much

Breads, Muffins & Butters

Bread is beautiful. The aroma of bread, baking in the oven, has stirred the hearts of poets and the minds of men. Perhaps no other single food is so steeped in the tradition and ceremony of so many peoples. Breaking bread and the Sabbath loaf is a sacred institution for centuries. Some people regard bread as holy and in Arabic, it literally means life.

Bread is beautiful because bread is the stuff legends are made of. Why not start a legend of your own with rich and glorious . . .

Heirloom Fruit & Nut Bread

1 pound glazed cherries
1 pound glazed mixed fruits
3 cups walnuts
1/2 cup flour

1/2 cup plus 1 tablespoon butter
1 1/2 cups sugar
3 eggs
1 1/4 cups flour
1 teaspoon baking powder
1/2 teaspoon baking soda (omit for light bread)
2 teaspoons vanilla
1 small orange, grated

Preheat oven to 275°. Grease and flour 6 aluminum foil baby loaf pans, 6 x 3½ x 2-inches. Cut fruits and nuts into small pieces. Combine fruits and nuts with 1/2 cup flour and toss to coat evenly. Set aside.

Cream butter with sugar until light and fluffy. Add eggs, one at a time, beating well after each addition. Gradually add the dry ingredients and beat for 2 minutes more. Add vanilla and grated orange and mix well.

Divide batter into the 6 prepared pans. Bake in a 275° oven for about 1 hour and 30 minutes or until a cake tester inserted in center comes out clean. Cool bread in pans, on a wire rack. While cooling, paint with sherry 2 or 3 times.

Pumpkin Raisin Nut Bread

1 cup canned pumpkin
1 1/8 cup sugar
1/2 cup orange juice
2 eggs
1/4 cup butter, softened (1/2 stick)

2 cups flour
2 teaspoons baking powder
1/2 teaspoon baking soda
1/2 teaspoon salt
1 teaspoon cinnamon
2 teaspoons pumpkin pie spice

1 cup raisins, plumped in orange juice and drained
1 cup chopped walnuts

In your mixer, beat together the pumpkin, sugar, orange juice, eggs and softened butter until well blended. Add the dry ingredients all at once, stirring until they are moistened. Stir by hand and do not overmix. Add the raisins and the walnuts and stir quickly until combined. Place mixture into 2 foil loaf pans, 4 x 8-inches, that have been lightly greased and floured. Bake in a preheated 350° oven for about 45 to 50 minutes or until a cake tester inserted in center comes out clean. Serve with Creamy Honey Butter and somehow things will never be the same. Makes 2 loaves 8 inches each.

Creamy Honey Butter

1/2 cup butter
1/4 cup orange honey
1/2 teaspoon orange extract

Beat butter until creamy and light. Add honey and orange extract and beat until fluffy. Taste at this point. If you like it sweeter, add a little more honey. Refrigerate. Remove from the refrigerator about 45 minutes before you are planning to serve it.

Note:
Place butter in a pretty crock and you have a lovely gift from your kitchen.

Banana Chocolate Chip Bread

1 1/2 cups flour

1 teaspoon soda
4 tablespoons sour cream

1/4 pound soft butter (1 stick)
1 1/4 cups sugar

2 eggs

1 cup mashed bananas (about 2 medium bananas)
1 bag (6 ounces) semi-sweet chocolate chips
pinch of salt
1 teaspoon vanilla

Sift flour three times and set aside. Mix together soda and sour cream and set aside. Cream butter with sugar until light and fluffy. Add eggs, one at a time, beating well after each addition. Add flour and sour cream mixture alternately to butter mixture. Stir in bananas and chocolate chips. Add vanilla and salt.

Place mixture in a greased and floured loaf pan and bake in a 350° oven for about 40-45 minutes or until a cake tester inserted in center comes out clean. (You can use 3 baby loaf pans, 6x3½-inches. Test at 35 minutes. I would recommend this if you are planning to store or freeze part of the bread.) Serve with sweet, creamy butter.

Apple Orange Bran Muffins

You will love these bran muffins. They are moist, fragrant and delicious.

2 cups Raisin Bran Cereal
3/4 cup milk
1 egg, beaten
1/4 cup (1/2 stick) softened butter

1 apple, peeled and grated
1 orange, grated (remove any large pieces of membrane, but use the peel, juice and pulp)

1 cup flour
2 1/2 teaspoons baking powder
1/2 teaspoon salt
1 1/2 teaspoons cinnamon
6 tablespoons sugar

Combine cereal, milk, egg and soft butter and mix well. Add the apple and the orange and stir to combine. Add all the dry ingredients at once and mix until mixture is moistened and even. Do not overmix. Immediately divide mixture among 12 paper muffin cups and place in muffin pan. Bake at 400° for 25 minutes or until a cake tester inserted in center comes out clean. Makes 12 muffins.

Orange Butter

1/2 cup butter (1 stick), unsalted and slightly softened. (If butter is too soft, it will become oily.)
1 cup sifted powdered sugar
1 teaspoon orange zest
1 teaspoon orange extract *or* 1 tablespoon orange liqueur

Cream butter until it is light. Slowly beat in powdered sugar, orange zest and orange flavoring. Place butter in a crock and refrigerate before serving. Makes about 1 cup flavored butter.

French Bread with Olive Oil, Garlic & Herbs

1 large French bread, cut in half lengthwise

olive oil, garlic powder, paprika and oregano

Baste cut side of French bread generously with olive oil. Sprinkle with garlic powder, paprika and oregano to taste. Cut slices into bread about 2/3 through. Wrap each half in foil and heat in a 350° oven until heated through.

French Bread with Garlic & Parmesan

1 French bread, cut into 3/4-inch slices

3/4 cup mayonnaise
2 cloves minced garlic
3/4 cup grated Parmesan cheese

paprika

Place cut slices of bread on a cookie sheet. Combine mayonnaise, garlic and grated cheese and mix until blended. Spread paste on rounds of French Bread. Sprinkle tops with paprika. Heat in a 350° oven until heated through. Broil for a few seconds to lightly brown. Serve with soup or salad.

Hors D'Oeuvres & Small Entrees

Mushrooms Stuffed with Crabmeat & Garlic Cream Cheese

This is one of the most delicious stuffings for mushrooms. I have probably received more letters praising this recipe than any other.

3/4 pound medium-sized mushrooms, cleaned and stems removed
1/2 pound crabmeat, pick over for bones
1/2 pound cream cheese
1/2 cup garlic croutons, finely crushed
Parmesan cheese, grated
paprika

Mix together the crabmeat, cream cheese and croutons until mixture is blended. Mound mixture into mushroom caps. Sprinkle tops generously with grated Parmesan cheese and lightly with paprika. Broil until piping hot. Make extras. They are especially good.

Chili Con Queso Ethel

1 tablespoon olive oil
1 clove garlic, mashed

1 can (4 ounces) diced green chiles
1 pound Kraft's Old English Cheese
1 can (1 pound) Italian tomatoes, drained. Cut tomatoes into little pieces.

Saute garlic in olive oil. Add remaining ingredients and simmer until the cheese is melted. Transfer the mixture to a heated chafing dish. Serve with crisp tortilla chips.

Crabmeat with Cream Cheese & Green Onions

1/2 pound cream cheese
4 tablespoons finely minced green onions (use only the tops.)
1/4 cup whipping cream
1 tablespoon lemon juice
1/3 cup toasted, slivered almonds
1/2 pound crabmeat, picked over for bones

Beat the cream cheese until light and fluffy. Add green onions, whipping cream and lemon juice and beat until blended. Mix in almonds and crabmeat. Serve with thin slices of black bread or French bread.

Note:
Can also be served warm. Heat in an oven-proof casserole at 350° until hot, no longer. Do not overcook.

Crabmeat with Curry

1/2 pound cream cheese
dash Worcestershire Sauce
dash of garlic powder
1/2 teaspoon curry powder
2 tablespoons cream

1/2 pound crabmeat, picked over for bones

Beat the cream cheese, Worcestershire Sauce, garlic powder, curry powder and cream until the mixture is light and fluffy. Add crabmeat and mix together. Place mixture into an oven-proof casserole and refrigerate. When ready to serve, place casserole in a 350° oven until heated through. Do not cook. Serve hot with crackers or thinly sliced bread.

Clams with Garlic & Herbs

3 cans minced clams (7 ounces each) drained. Reserve
  juice.
1 package prepared herbed stuffing
1/4 pound butter, melted
2 cloves garlic, minced
1 teaspoon Italian Herb Seasoning
1 tablespoon chopped parsley
3 tablespoons finely minced onion
6 tablespoons grated Parmesan cheese
salt and pepper to taste

Combine all the ingredients and toss until well mixed.
Now, slowly add the reserved clam broth until the
stuffing holds together and is moist. Do not let filling
get soggy or stay too dry. Divide mixture between 12
clam shells. Sprinkle with paprika and a pinch of
oregano.

Place clam shells on a cookie sheet and heat in a 350°
oven until piping hot. Brown under the broiler for a
few seconds until golden. Serves 12 as a first course.

Cold Vegetable Platter with Sauce Verte

Arrange a large platter of sliced carrots, celery, cucumbers, zucchini, mushrooms, cherry tomatoes, jicama, etc. in any combination you desire. Slice the vegetables straight, on the diagonal, into circles, sticks, curls, etc. Arrange on a bed of lettuce. Dip the ends of the lettuce leaves in paprika for a pretty effect. Place the Imperial Sauce Verte in the center and Voila! you have a party.

Many friends have said that my Sauce Verte is the best they have ever tasted. I hope you enjoy it too.

Imperial Sauce Verte

1/2 cup frozen spinach, defrosted and drained

3 springs parsley, stems removed, use only the leaves
2 green onions, use the green tops and the white bulbs
1 cup mayonnaise
1/2 cup sour cream
1 1/2 tablespoons lemon juice
salt to taste

Place spinach in strainer and drain liquid. Set aside. Place remaining ingredients in blender and blend at high speed until smooth. Combine spinach and blended ingredients and mix well. Refrigerate until ready to use. Makes 2 cups.

Meatballs in Sweet & Sour Cranberry Sauce

1 1/2 pounds ground beef
1 package dehydrated onion soup
2 eggs
1/2 cup herb seasoned stuffing mix, soaked in
3 tablespoons water
2 tablespoons dried parsley flakes
salt and pepper to taste

Combine all the ingredients and shape into 1/2-inch balls. Brown the meatballs in a large skillet, shaking the pan frequently so that the meatballs will brown on all sides. If the meat is very lean, do this in a little butter. Place meatballs and hot Sweet and Sour Cranberry Sauce in a chafing dish. Makes about 50 to 60 meatballs.

Sweet & Sour Cranberry Sauce

1 cup cranberry sauce, whole berry
1/2 cup ketchup
2 tablespoons grated onion
1 teaspoon vinegar
2 tablespoons brown sugar

Combine all the ingredients and simmer over low heat for 15 to 20 minutes. Add meatballs and heat through.

Pork Won Tons
with Currant Mustard Sauce

1 package prepared won ton skins (about 45-50 in package)

1/2 pound ground pork
1/4 pound minced mushrooms
1/4 cup finely minced green onions
6 water chestnuts, finely minced
salt and pepper to taste
pinch of garlic powder
pinch of MSG (optional)
2 tablespoons oil

Heat oil in skillet. Add all the ingredients except the won ton skins and stir fry until pork is thoroughly cooked.

Place 1 teaspoon of filling on each skin. Moisten edges and fold in half, either lengthwise or on the diagonal. Run fingers around the edges to seal. Fry filled won tons in hot oil until golden brown. Turn and brown other side. Serve hot with Plum Sauce or Currant Mustard Sauce for dipping.

Currant Mustard Sauce

1 cup currant jelly
1/4 cup prepared mustard
1/2 cup currants, (dried)

Heat together all the ingredients and simmer for about 5 minutes. Makes about 1 1/2 cups sauce.

Batter-Fried Shrimp with Hot Plum Sauce

2 pounds shrimp, shelled and deveined

1/2 cup flour
1/2 cup corn starch
5/6 cup cold water
1 egg
1/8 teaspoon salt
1/8 teaspoon MSG

Lightly dust shrimp with flour. With a rotary beater, mix together the flour, corn starch, water, egg, salt and MSG. Beat until thoroughly smooth.

Dip shrimp in batter and fry in hot oil. When lightly browned on one side, turn and fry the other side. Remove from oil and drain. Keep warm. Serve with Hot Plum Sauce for dipping. Serves 4.

Hot Plum Sauce

1/2 cup plum preserves
2 tablespoons brown sugar
2 tablespoons vinegar
2 tablespoons ketchup

Combine all the ingredients and cook for 5 minutes. Allow to cool a few minutes and serve. Makes about 3/4 cup sauce.

Casseroles

Paella Darling

This is a very delicious, jiffy paella, that makes left-over chicken or turkey festive enough for a dinner party.

3 cups cooked chicken or turkey, cut into large dice

2 large onions, chopped
3 tablespoons oil
1 can, 4 ounces, Ortega diced green chiles
2 tomatoes, chopped coarsely

1 1/2 cups raw rice
1 can Campbell's Chicken Broth, dilute with 1/4 cup water
salt and pepper to taste
3 sprinkles cumin
1/4 teaspoon tumeric

Cut chicken into large pieces and set aside. Saute onions in oil until onions are tender. Do not brown. Add chile, tomatoes and chicken and heat through. Add remaining ingredients, cover and cook over low heat until rice is tender and liquid is absorbed. Stir and serve hot. Serves 6.

Note:
This is the basic recipe. You can add hot, buttered peas over the top. An excellent addition is to toss in 1/2 pound of shrimp that were sauteed in butter and garlic for a few minutes. Do this just before serving. Shrimp can overcook easily and become rubbery. You can add lobster, clams, etc. Just be certain that your casserole is reheated, then add hot shrimp, etc. Of course, the casserole is excellent in its basic form.

Eggplant Lasagna Greenfield

This superb eggplant recipe was given to me by a friend but it used almost 1 cup of olive oil. I have modified the technique and the amounts out of deference to those who are counting calories. Instead of frying the eggplant, I bake it. This is easier and uses practically no oil. I believe you will find the end result lighter and more delicious.

2 large eggplants
salt and pepper

2 eggs, beaten
1 pound Ricotta cheese
3/4 pound Mozzarella cheese, cubed
1/2 cup grated Parmesan cheese
1/2 teaspoon dried basil

3 cups Hunts Herbed Tomato Sauce (about 1 1/2 cans)

Peel and slice eggplant in 1/4-inch slices. Sprinkle with salt and pepper. Place eggplant slices on a lightly greased cookie sheet, brush lightly with oil, cover with foil and bake in a 400° oven for about 15 minutes or until eggplant slices are soft. Remove from oven and set aside.

Combine eggs, cheeses and basil and mix together until blended. Set aside.

Grease a 9x13-inch lasagna pan or cook and serve casserole. Now, layer tomato sauce, eggplant and cheese mixture in prepared casserole, starting and ending with the tomato sauce. Sprinkle top with additional Parmesan cheese.

Bake at 375° for about 40-45 minutes or until piping hot. Serves 6 to 8.

Cabbage Rolls in Sweet & Sour Tomato Sauce

2 large cabbage heads

2 pounds lean ground beef
1 cup raw rice
1 package onion soup mix
2 eggs
1/2 cup cold water
1/8 teaspoon garlic powder
salt and pepper to taste

Wash cabbage and remove the core. Stand it up and cook it in boiling water for 10 to 12 minutes. Remove and refresh under cold water. Carefully remove the outer leaves. When the leaves get too small to roll, chop them finely and place them in a large Dutch-oven-type casserole.

Combine all the ingredients except the cabbage and mix until blended. Place about 2 tablespoons meat mixture on bottom of cabbage leaf. Tuck in the sides and roll it. Place rolls in Dutch oven. Pour Sweet and Sour Tomato Sauce over the rolls and cook, covered, for about 1 1/2 hours over low heat. Makes about 24 cabbage rolls.

Sweet & Sour Tomato Sauce

2 tablespoons oil
1 can (1 pound 12 ounces) stewed tomatoes, chopped
2 cans (8 ounces, each) tomato sauce
1 can (10 1/2 ounces) beef broth
6 tablespoons lemon juice
2 tablespoons brown sugar
3 tablespoons sugar
salt and pepper to taste

Combine all the ingredients and mix until blended.

Noodle Lasagna Italienne

3/4 pound wide egg noodles, cooked and drained

1 onion, finely chopped
1 tablespoon oil
1 pound ground beef
1 can (1 pound 12 ounces) stewed tomatoes, cut into
  small pieces
1 can (6 ounces) tomato paste
1 teaspoon sugar
1 teaspoon Italian Herb Seasoning
salt and pepper to taste

1 pound Ricotto cheese
3 eggs
1/2 cup grated Parmesan cheese

Saute onion in oil until onion is soft. Add ground
beef and continue sauteing, crumbling the beef, until
beef is cooked through. Add tomatoes, tomato paste,
sugar and seasonings and simmer gently for 20 minutes. Set sauce aside.

Beat together the Ricotto cheese, eggs and grated
cheese.

Spread a thin layer of sauce in an 8x12-inch lasagna
pan. Place half the noodles over the sauce. Follow
with half the cheese mixture and half the sauce.
Repeat, layering the remaining noodles, cheese mixture and sauce. Sprinkle top generously with additional grated Parmesan cheese.

Bake casserole in a 350° oven for about 35 minutes
or until piping hot. Serves 6.

Note:
*Entire casserole can be assembled earlier in the day
and refrigerated. When reheating, allow to come to
room temperature and heat as described above.*

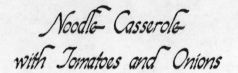

Noodle Casserole with Tomatoes and Onions

1/2 pound wide noodles, cooked and drained
1/4 cup butter, (1/2 stick), melted

1 can (1 pound 12 ounces) sliced tomatoes, drained
1/2 cup of drained tomato juice
8 green onions, finely minced
3 cloves garlic, pressed or mashed
2 tablespoons parsley leaves (fresh), chopped
salt and pepper to taste

1/4 cup butter, melted
1 pound Jack cheese, grated
1/4 cup Parmesan cheese, grated

Cook noodles al dente (tender but still firm). Toss noodles in first 1/4 cup melted butter. Set aside.

Combine tomatoes, juice, onions, garlic, parsley, salt and pepper. (If you cannot find the large can of sliced tomatoes, buy the whole tomatoes and slice them thin.)

In a lovely heat and serve casserole, brush some melted butter. Layer 1/2 the noodles, 1/2 the tomato mixture and 1/2 of the cheeses. Drizzle a little of the melted butter and repeat the layers, ending with the cheese. Drizzle a little more butter over the top.

Heat in a 350° oven until heated through. Serves 6 for lunch.

Casserole with Apples, Raisins and Walnuts

6 eggs, well beaten
3 tablespoons flour
3 tablespoons sugar
1/2 cup cream
1 teaspoon vanilla

2 apples, peeled, cored and grated
1/2 cup golden raisins, plumped in orange juice, drained
1/2 cup chopped walnuts
1 teaspoon orange zest

3 tablespoons butter
3 tablespoons cinnamon sugar

Beat eggs with flour, sugar, cream and vanilla until light. Add apples, raisins, walnuts and orange zest and mix well.

Melt butter in a 12-inch baking pan or oval baker. Add egg mixture to pan and sprinkle top with cinnamon sugar. Bake in a 350° oven for about 50 minutes or until eggs are set and top is golden brown. Serve with a dollup of sour cream and a tablespoonful of defrosted strawberry slices in syrup. Serves 4.

Note:
This is exceptionally good served with Creme Vanilla instead of the sour cream.
I have not found it satisfactory to assemble this dish earlier in the day.

31

French Mushroom Onion Quiche

2 9-inch frozen pie shells (Buy the shallow shells, not
the deep dish variety)

1 pound mushrooms, cleaned and sliced
1 large onion, chopped
1/4 cup butter (1/2 stick)

3 eggs
1 1/2 cups half and half cream
1/2 cup Parmesan cheese
salt and pepper to taste

Bake frozen pie shells at 400° for about 10 minutes
or until lightly golden.

Saute mushrooms and onion in butter until onions
are tender. Divide mixture evenly between the 2
pie shells.

Beat together the eggs and the cream for 2 minutes
at medium speed. Add the Parmesan cheese, salt and
pepper and mix well. Divide mixture evenly between
the 2 pie shells.

Bake in a 350° oven for 40 to 45 minutes or until
custard is set and top is golden. Each pie serves 4.

Note:
*This quiche freezes beautifully so you can serve one
and freeze the other. Excellent for lunch or as a first
course for dinner.*

Soups

I often wonder what it is about soup that is so endearing to the hearts of men. Breathes there a man with soul so dead, who hasn't heard or hasn't said . . . something about Mama's unbelievable chicken soup with the dumplings that floated on top . . . or Grandma's delicious barley soup that was so thick a spoon could stand up straight in the middle . . . or Aunt Amy's indescribable vegetable soup with the alphabets that spelled your name.

What is it about soup that lingers so long in the memory? Chances are that these lovely ladies were great cooks in many ways. But somehow, the warmth, the loving quality of soup is what we choose to remember with nostalgia.

The essence of soup is its broth and if you don't have homemade stock on hand, there are a variety of substitutes you can use. Chicken or beef seasoned stock bases are good. Canned broths can be sparkled with a little champagne or white wine. Using them undiluted makes your soup robust and hearty. Of course, if you have the time, homemade soups and stocks are wonderful. But the prepared broths and stock bases work very well, too.

Zucchini Soup Darling

6 medium zucchini, do not peel, slice with skin
2 large onions, sliced
1/3 bunch parsley, use the leaves and discard the
    stems
1 tablespoon dried shallots
2 tablespoons butter
2 tablespoons olive oil

1 can (10 1/2 ounces) Campbell's Chicken Broth,
    undiluted

2 potatoes, peeled, boiled and very finely chopped
1 pint half and half

salt and pepper to taste
pinch of garlic powder
pinch of dried dill weed

Combine first 6 ingredients and saute slowly until
vegetables are tender. Do not brown. Place these vegetables into a blender container and blend with some
of the chicken broth until vegetables are pureed and
smooth.

Pour mixture into a saucepan, add the remaining
chicken broth, potatoes and half and half. Add salt,
pepper, garlic powder and dill. Heat through and
simmer for 5 minutes. Serves 6 with pride.

Note:
*Soup can be made a day earlier and refrigerated.
Remove from the refrigerator about 30 minutes
before you are planning to reheat it. Reheat carefully over low heat.*
*Serve soup with the wonderful little Herbed Croutons
served on the side.*

Clam Chowder Darling

1 large onion, finely chopped or grated
2 tablespoons butter
1 teaspoon flour
8 strips of bacon, cooked, drained and crumbled
1 can minced clams (8 ounces)
1 cup bottled clam juice
1/2 teaspoon basil
pinch of thyme
1 cup heavy cream
1 small potato, peeled, boiled and very finely chopped
salt and white pepper to taste

Saute onion in butter until onion is tender. Add flour and cook for a minute or two. Add the remaining ingredients and simmer gently for about 10 minutes. Serve with Cheese Straws. Serves 4.

Note:
Soup can be made earlier in the day and refrigerated. Allow soup to come to room temperature and then reheat.

Chicken Soup with Instant Noodles

2 cans (10 1/2 ounces each) chicken soup
1 can (10 1/2 ounces) water
1 teaspoon chicken seasoned stock base

3 eggs
3 tablespoons flour, sifted
pinch of salt and white pepper

1 tablespoon dried chopped chives
salt and pepper to taste

Bring to boil the chicken broth, water and stock base. Beat together the eggs, flour and pinch of salt and pepper until the mixture is blended.

Slowly and in a steady stream, trickle the egg mixture into the boiling broth. Add chopped chives and salt and pepper to taste. Lower heat and simmer soup for 5 minutes. Serve with toasted rounds of French Bread with Garlic and Parmesan. Serves 6.

Beef Barley Mushroom Soup

2 cans (10 1/2 ounces each) beef broth
1 can (10 1/2 ounces) water
1 teaspoon beef seasoned stock base

1 onion, finely chopped
1 carrot, grated
1/2 cup pearl barley

1/2 pound mushrooms
2 tablespoons butter

1 cup leftover roast beef, cut into small pieces
1 tablespoon chopped parsley
salt and pepper to taste

In a large saucepan place beef broth, water, stock base, onion, carrot and barley and simmer mixture until barley is cooked, about 1 hour. Meanwhile, saute mushrooms in butter until they are tender.

Add mushrooms to the soup along with the roast beef and chopped parsley. Adjust salt and pepper. Add a little beef broth if soup is too thick. Serve with some crusty black pumpernickel and sweet whipped butter.

Salads

&

Dressings

If the incomparable Caesar is one of your preferred salads, why not master the art of making it, so that you can serve it soon to your family or friends. Set a few simple ingredients on a tray and in a large wooden salad bowl, gently roll and turn the salad to masterful perfection and with a grand flourish, right at the table.

While you are doing this, you might tell the legend of how this magnificent salad is believed to have been created from some soup greens (romaine) in the kitchen. It seems that this Master Chef called Caesar was expecting a grand crowd for dinner, but it was late and his cupboards were depleted and all he had on hand were the few simple ingredients for the salad. After some tasting and adjusting and tasting, this monochromatic salad was born.

But before you begin, here are a few simple precepts to keep in mind. First, you must use romaine lettuce, which has been washed, dried and chilled. Tear it into bite-size pieces, please, for more carefree dining. It is a bother to fuss with over-size pieces of lettuce. You can substitute grated Parmesan cheese for the Romano cheese.

Anchovies are often used in making the salad, but the classic recipe does not include them. Gently turn the lettuce leaves in the dressing so that they are completely coated. Pick up a leaf and examine it. It should not be drippy wet, nor patchy dry. And after the ceremony, listen as they HAIL the mighty Caesar.

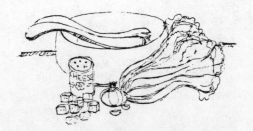

The Incomparable Salad Caesar

2 heads Romaine lettuce, washed, dried and broken into bite-sized pieces

6 tablespoons oil. (You can use 3 tablespoons olive oil and 3 tablespoons salad oil.)
1 tablespoon wine vinegar
3 tablespoons fresh lemon juice
1/2 cup grated Romano cheese
1/2 teaspoon salt or to taste
freshly ground pepper to taste
1 clove garlic, put through a garlic press

6 filets of anchovies, minced (optional)

1 egg, coddled. (Simmer egg for 1 minute in gently boiling water. Remove and run under cold water.)

1 cup prepared garlic croutons. (You can make croutons by cutting 6 slices of French or Italian bread into 1/2-inch squares. Saute bread cubes in olive oil or butter with 1 clove crushed garlic until they are crisp and golden.)

Beat oil with a wire whisk. Continue beating, adding the vinegar, lemon juice, grated cheese, salt, pepper, garlic and anchovies. Add lettuce and toss gently. Add coddled egg and continue tossing carefully until the lettuce leaves are completely coated. Add croutons and toss to combine them. Serve at once so that the croutons do not get soggy. Serves 6.

Tomatoes Deborah

3 tomatoes, cut into slices
2 tablespoons dried toasted onion flakes
1 teaspoon dried parsley flakes
6 tablespoons salad oil
3 tablespoons white wine vinegar
3/4 teaspoon salt
1/2 to 1 clove garlic, minced
4 tablespoons grated Parmesan cheese

Place the tomatoes in a lovely glass serving bowl. Combine the remaining ingredients and mix well. Pour dressing over the tomatoes and marinate for at least 4 hours. Serves 4.

Note:
This is a marvellous little salad, that I hope you enjoy. Make it in the morning and serve it at dinner.

Cucumbers in Sour Cream

3 cucumbers, peeled and thinly sliced
1 teaspoon salt

1 teaspoon sugar
1/8 teaspoon pepper
1 tablespoon lemon juice
2 tablespoons vinegar
1 cup sour cream
3 tablespoons chopped chives

Sprinkle cucumbers with salt. Weigh them down with a heavy plate and refrigerate them for an hour or two. Rinse the slices and squeeze them dry.

Combine the remaining ingredients and pour over the cucumber slices. Refrigerate. Serve chilled. Garnish with chopped chives. Serves 6.

Salad Dressing Joseph

This is a marvellous little dressing. It is delicate and delicious. Serve it on salad greens, tomatoes or cucumbers.

1 cup mayonnaise
1/2 cup sour cream
3 sprigs parsley (remove stems)
2 green onions, whole
1 1/2 tablespoons fresh lemon juice
salt and pepper to taste

Place all the ingredients in a blender jar and blend at high speed until onions and parsley are fully incorporated and smooth, about 1 minute. Makes 1 1/2 cups dressing.

Note:
Dressing will keep in the refrigerator for at least 1 week.

Green Goddess Dressing Darling

This salad dressing is also exceptionally good as a dip for a cold vegetable platter.

1 cup mayonnaise
1/4 cup cream
1 teaspoon garlic powder
1/4 bunch parsley, remove stems, use only the leaves
3 green onions, medium-sized, use the whole onion
1/4 teaspoon MSG or Accent
salt to taste

Combine all the ingredients in blender container and blend at high speed until mixture is smooth. Pour dressing into a glass jar, cover and refrigerate. Makes 1 1/2 cups.

Note:
Dressing will keep for a week in the refrigerator.

Mushroom Salad Darling

1 egg yolk
1/4 cup red wine vinegar
2 tablespoons red wine
2 tablespoons Dijon-style mustard
1 tablespoon chopped chives
1 tablespoon chopped parsley
1 teaspoon sugar
salt and pepper to taste

1 cup peanut oil

1 pound mushrooms, cleaned, stems removed and
   sliced thin

In blender container, place egg yolk, vinegar, wine,
mustard, chives, parsley, sugar, salt and pepper.
Blend for 30 seconds.

Now add oil in a steady trickle, blending at high
speed until dressing is creamy and oil is thoroughly
incorporated. Pour about 1 cup dressing over the
mushrooms and toss until the mushrooms are completely coated. Sprinkle with some chopped chives
and serve at once. Makes 1 1/2 cups dressing.

Note:
Dressing can be made ahead and stored in a jar for
about 1 week in the refrigerator.

Bacon Tomato Salad Jeffrey

4 tomatoes, cut into small pieces. (If you have the time, it would be just lovely to skin the tomatoes.)
16 slices bacon, cooked, crisped and crumpled
1 onion, finely minced
4 hard boiled eggs, coarsely chopped

Combine all the ingredients and toss to mix well. Serve with Jeffrey's Special Dressing at time of serving. Serves 4.

Jeffrey's Special Dressing

1/2 cup oil
1/4 cup vinegar
1/2 cup ketchup
1/4 cup grated Parmesan cheese
2 tablespoons sugar, scanty
1 teaspoon lemon juice
1 tablespoon water

Place all the ingredients in a jar with a lid that can screw on tightly. Shake vigorously. Refrigerate dressing until ready to serve. Makes about 1 1/2 cups dressing.

Note:
Dressing can be made ahead and refrigerated for several days.

Grandma Stella's Potato Salad

8 medium-sized potatoes, scrubbed and tubbed
3 carrots, grated
6 green onions, finely chopped. (Use the whole onion)
2 tablespoons sugar
3 tablespoons vinegar
1 teaspoon salt or to taste
pepper, optional
1 cup mayonnaise, about

Cook the potatoes, unpeeled, in boiling water until they are tender. Do not overcook. Peel and cut them into small pieces. (I find slicing more satisfactory than cubing.)

Combine potatoes, carrots and green onions. Sprinkle with sugar, vinegar and salt and toss to coat evenly. (Important!) Let mixture rest for 10 minutes. Now add sufficient mayonnaise to coat potatoes. Mix well and refrigerate. Garnish with some finely chopped green onion and carrot curls. Serves 6.

Cucumbers with Dill Dressing

1 cup sour cream
1/2 cup mayonnaise
3 tablespoons fresh lemon juice
2 tablespoons chopped chives
1 tablespoon fresh dill weed or 1 teaspoon dried dill weed
salt and white pepper to taste

3 cucumbers, thinly sliced

Combine all the ingredients except the cucumbers. Place dressing in a glass jar with a lid and refrigerate it. Pour dressing over the cucumbers when serving. Makes about 2 cups.

Fish
&
Shellfish

Crabmeat with Shrimp Sauce

3 egg yolks
1 1/2 tablespoons lemon juice
pinch of salt and white pepper

3/4 cup butter (1 1/2 sticks)

1/4 pound baby shrimp, cooked

1 pound cooked crabmeat, picked over for bones

Place the egg yolks, lemon juice, salt and pepper in a blender container. Blend for 10 seconds at high speed.

Heat butter until it is sizzling hot and bubbly, but be careful not to brown it. Add the hot, sizzling butter very slowly, in a steady stream, while the blender continues running at high speed. When the butter is completely incorporated, sauce is ready. Add the baby shrimp, and pour the sauce evenly over the cooked crabmeat. Broil until lightly colored, about 1 minute. Serves 4 or 5.

Curried Shrimp with Lemon Sauce

3 egg yolks
2 tablespoons cream
1 1/2 tablespoons lemon juice
1/2 teaspoon finely grated lemon peel
3/4 teaspoon curry powder
2 packages (3 ounces each) cream cheese
salt and white pepper to taste

1 pound cooked shrimp

In your electric mixer, beat together all the ingredients except the shrimp until they are light and fluffy. Place mixture on the top of a double boiler over hot water and heat, stirring until mixture is warm.

Place shrimp in a shallow, oval server. Spread sauce evenly over the shrimp and broil until lightly colored. Serve with Rice with Raisins and Almonds. Serves 4.

Shrimp in Ramekins with Swiss Cheese and Tomatoes

1/2 pound mushrooms, sliced
2 tablespoons butter
2 tablespoons flour
1 cup half and half
pinch of dry mustard
salt and pepper to taste

1 pound cooked shrimp

4 slices, (1 ounce each) Swiss cheese
4 very thin slices tomatoes
4 teaspoons chopped chives

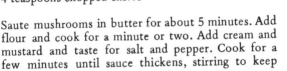

Saute mushrooms in butter for about 5 minutes. Add flour and cook for a minute or two. Add cream and mustard and taste for salt and pepper. Cook for a few minutes until sauce thickens, stirring to keep sauce smooth.

Divide shrimp between 4 ramekins. Divide sauce evenly over shrimp. Top each ramekin with a slice of Swiss cheese, a slice of tomato and 1 teaspoon chopped chives. Heat in a 350° oven until heated through. Put under the broiler for few seconds to brown cheese. Serves 4. Serve with baby buttered potatoes.

Note:
This is a delightful little dish that can be assembled and cooked in literally a few minutes.
Mushroom sauce can be made earlier in the day.
Entire dish can be assembled earlier in the day and heated at time of serving.
When you reheat, make certain not to overcook. Simply heat through, broil and serve.

Shrimp in Lemon Butter Sauce

2 pounds raw shrimp, peeled and deveined. Sprinkle with salt, white pepper and dust lightly with flour.

1/4 cup olive oil
1/4 cup (1/2 stick) butter, melted
3 tablespoons lemon juice
4 cloves garlic, mashed or put through a garlic press

In a round or oval au gratin baker, combine all the ingredients. Turn and toss to coat shrimp evenly. Broil shrimp about 6-inches from the heat for about 8 minutes or until they turn pink, no longer. Turn shrimp twice during broiling time.

Remove shrimp from oven and sprinkle top with Garlic Crumbs. Broil for another minute or until topping is golden. Serves 6.

Garlic Crumbs

1/4 cup Ritz cracker crumbs
1/4 cup grated Parmesan cheese
1 tablespoon minced parsley
1 clove garlic, put through a garlic press
2 tablespoons melted butter

Combine all the ingredients and toss to thoroughly mix.

Lobster Newburgh

2 tablespoons butter
3 egg yolks, lightly beaten
1 cup cream *or* 1 cup half and half
1/4 pound cream cheese, softened
3 tablespoons grated Parmesan cheese
1 tablespoon dry white wine
1/2 teaspoon paprika
pinch of dry mustard
salt and pepper to taste

6 halved, cooked lobster tails, about 6 ounces each.
  Remove meat and cut into large pieces.

In top of a double boiler, place butter, yolks, cream
and cream cheese. Cook over low heat, stirring con-
stantly until sauce thickens and coats a spoon. Add
Parmesan cheese, wine, paprika, pinch of dry mustard,
salt and pepper to taste. Add lobster meat and heat
through. Fill reserved shells with lobster and sauce.
Sprinkle with buttered bread crumbs and broil for a
few seconds to brown. Garnish with parsley. Serves 6.
Serve with Parsleyed Noodles with Green Onions.

Note:
Be careful not to use high heat as sauce can curdle.

Filets of Sole
with Tomato Cheese Sauce

2 pounds filets of sole, sprinkle lightly with salt

2 tablespoons olive oil
2 tablespoons melted butter
2 cloves garlic, finely minced
1/2 pound grated Mozzarella cheese

2 cups Tomato Cheese Sauce *or* 1 can (16 ounces)
   Herbed Tomato Sauce

In a 12x16-inch pan, lay the filets flat in one layer.
Heat together the oil, butter and garlic and drizzle
this mixture evenly over the filets. Broil the filets for
about 5 or 6 minutes. Do not overcook.

Ladle Tomato Cheese Sauce over the filets and then
sprinkle the grated Mozzarella evenly over all. Broil
for another minute or so until sauce is hot and cheese
is melted and browned. Serves 6.

Tomato Cheese Sauce

1 can (1 pound 12 ounces) stewed tomatoes, pureed
   in blender
1 can tomato paste (6 ounces)
2 tablespoons sugar
2 tablespoons olive oil
1/2 teaspoon Italian Herb Seasoning
2 tablespoons dried onion flakes
salt and pepper to taste
1/2 cup grated Parmesan cheese

Combine all the ingredients and simmer for about 15
minutes. Makes about 4 cups sauce.

Note:
Sauce can be frozen.

Meats

Good friends and informal dinners go together like love and marriage. What can smoothen a crinkle in the spirit better than sitting around a table with some intimate friends, exchanging a few lively ideas and enjoying a country-style dinner with several hearty, robust dishes, a loaf of hot, crusty French bread and a flask of a full-bodied wine. Add a few fresh flowers, a candle or two and the pleasure will linger long after dinner is over. Country Style Pot Roast is a grand dish for just such occasions.

Country Style Pot Roast

4 pounds brisket of beef, lean and trimmed. Sprinkle
  with salt, pepper and garlic powder

1 envelope dry Onion Soup Mix
1 can beer, 12 ounces
1/2 cup ketchup
1/2 can Cranberry Sauce Whole Berry, (use 8 ounces)

Season brisket with salt, pepper and garlic powder. Place meat in a Dutch oven or roasting pan. Mix the onion soup mix, beer, ketchup and cranberry sauce together and pour mixture over the brisket. Cover and bake in a 350° oven until fork tender, about 2 hours. Remove from the oven and allow to cool.

Slice meat and return to pan with gravy, from which all the fat has been removed. When ready to serve, heat in a 350° oven, covered, for about 30 minutes or until heated through. Serves 6.

Note:
Gravy is delicious and does not need to be thickened. Entire dish can be prepared the day before and reheated at the time of serving with excellent results. Serve with Mushroom Rice and Cranberry Tangerine Mold as excellent accompaniments.

Easiest and Best Hungarian Goulash

2 pounds sirloin steak (Ask butcher to cut it in 1x1/8-inch pieces.)
2 tablespoons Dijon-style mustard

2 onions, chopped fine
2 tablespoons butter, plus additional butter for sauteing meat
2 tablespoons brown sugar
1/4 cup ketchup
1 teaspoon Bovril, Broth and Seasoning Base
1/2 cup white wine
2 tablespoons paprika

1 1/2 cups sour cream

Toss meat with mustard to coat evenly. Set aside.

Saute onions in 2 tablespoons butter and sugar until onions are golden. Add ketchup. Bovril, wine and paprika and cook until wine is reduced, about 5 minutes. Set aside.

Saute meat in additional very hot butter for a few minutes until meat loses its pinkness. Meat is very tender. Do not overcook.

Add meat to onion mixture. Add salt and pepper to taste. Just before serving, add sour cream and heat through. Serve on a bed of buttered noodles. Serves 6.

Easiest and Best Beef Stroganoff

2 pounds sirloin steak (Ask butcher to cut it for Stroganoff.)
2 tablespoons Grey Poupon Dijon-Style Mustard

4 shallots, finely chopped
1/2 pound mushrooms, cleaned and sliced
2 tablespoons butter
1 1/2 teaspoons flour
1/4 cup white wine
salt and pepper to taste

1 1/2 cups sour cream

Toss the meat with the mustard to coat evenly. Set aside.

Saute shallots in butter for a few minutes until golden. Add mushrooms and saute until mushrooms are lightly browned. Add the flour. Toss and cook the mushrooms with the flour for a minute or two. Add the wine and cook for a few minutes longer. Set aside.

Saute meat in additional very hot butter for a few minutes until meat loses its pinkness. Meat is very tender. Do not overcook.

Combine meat and mushroom mixture. Add salt and pepper to taste. Just before serving, add the sour cream and heat through. Serve on a bed of buttered noodles. Serves 6.

Note:
This is a marvellous little dish that is great for company and yet easy enough to make at the last minute, when you've had a busy day.
Entire dish can be made earlier in the day with the exception of adding the sour cream. Add the sour cream and heat through just before serving.

Meat Loaf in Raisin Sauce

1 1/2 pounds ground beef
1 cup herbed stuffing mix, soaked in 1/2 cup milk
2 eggs, beaten
1 tablespoon chopped parsley
1 teaspoon Bovril, Meat Extract Base
salt and pepper to taste

1 onion, finely chopped
1 tablespoon butter

In a large bowl, mix together the first six ingredients.
Saute onion in butter until it is soft and add it to
meat mixture. Place mixture in a 9x5-inch loaf pan.
Pour Raisin Sauce over the top. Bake in a 350° oven
for about 1 hour. Serves 4 or 5.

Raisin Sauce

1/2 cup currant jelly
1/2 cup chili sauce
2 tablespoons black currants
1/2 teaspoon mustard

Combine all the ingredients in a saucepan and heat
through until currant jelly is melted and mixture is
blended.

When the days turn warm suddenly, all at once, my thoughts gypsy to the sweet outdoors ... to a picnic in the park ... a banquet at the beach or a feast in a rolling meadow.

Plain or fancy, dining outdoors on a glorious day is a time of wonder for me. For the children, it is a time to be free ... to cast off their shoes and to feel the sun or the sand or the sea.

And, of course, sooner or later, (mostly sooner) all heads lightly turn to thoughts of food. For your next picnic, why not try a delectable tenderloin of beef, roasted to rare perfection and ladled with some exquisite Bearnaise Sauce. The Bearnaise Sauce is trouble-free, for it is kept ready and perfect in a Thermos-type jar.

And certainly, the Tenderloin of Beef with Bearnaise Sauce is marvellous for a dinner party too.

Tenderloin of Beef with Bearnaise Sauce

3 pound tenderloin of beef, rubbed with cut, fresh garlic, sprinkled with salt and pepper and brushed with 2 tablespoons melted butter

Roast tenderloin of beef in a preheated 400° oven for about 30 minutes for rare, but use a meat thermometer for accuracy. Allow to stand for about 5 minutes, cut into slices and serve. Ladle with Bearnaise Sauce.

Bearnaise Sauce

3 egg yolks
1 1/2 tablespoons lemon juice
pinch of salt
pinch of white pepper
1 tablespoon tarragon vinegar
1 teaspoon dried chopped parsley
1 tablespoon dried shredded green onions
1/4 teaspoon dried tarragon or to taste

3/4 cup butter

Place all the ingredients, except the butter in the blender container. Blend for 10 seconds at high speed.

Heat butter until it is sizzling hot and bubbly but be careful not to brown it. Add the hot, sizzling butter very slowly, in a steady stream, while the blender continues running at high speed. When the butter is completely incorporated, sauce will be thick and ready to serve. Makes about 1 cup.

Imperial Lamb Roast

1 leg of lamb, about 7 pounds (Ask butcher to bone, roll and tie it.)

1/4 cup oil
1/3 cup vinegar
1 teaspoon garlic powder
1 teaspoon salt
pepper to taste

Place lamb in a large bowl. Combine oil, vinegar, garlic powder, salt and pepper and pour mixture over the lamb. Marinate the lamb in the refrigerator for 24 hours, turning now and again.

Place lamb in a roasting pan with half the marinade. Roast in a preheated 425° oven for 20 minutes. Lower temperature to 350° and continue roasting. Allow about 20 minutes per pound for well-done. (Use a meat thermometer if you like it rarer.) Baste frequently with the additional marinade.

Remove meat from pan and strain the gravy. Remove excess fat. Combine 1 teaspoon cornstarch with 3 tablespoons cold water and add this to the strained meat juices. Heat it until it has thickened. Adjust seasonings.

Slice lamb and drizzle some sauce over the meat. Serve the remaining sauce in a sauce boat. Serves 8.

Note:
This marinade is also delicious for Shish Kabobs.

Roast Tenderloin of Pork with Apples & Honey Sauce

2 tenderloins of pork, (about 1 1/2 pounds each),
sprinkle with salt, pepper and garlic powder

Lawry's Teriyaki Marinade

Place the tenderloin of pork in a shallow roasting pan.
Roast in a preheated 350° oven for about 30 minutes,
basting frequently with Teriyaki Marinade. Then
baste every 15 minutes with Apples and Honey Sauce
until meat is tender and meat thermometer registers
175°, about another 40 minutes. Serve over rice or
with oriental noodles. Serves 8.

Apple & Honey Sauce

1 cup apple juice
1 apple, peeled, cored and grated
1/2 cup honey
1 teaspoon ginger
1/2 cup apple jelly

Combine all the ingredients and cook for a few
minutes until heated through and honey and apple
jelly are melted and well incorporated. Use to baste
the pork.

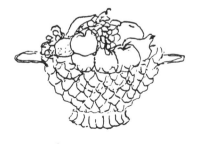

This is a wonderful little veal dish that I am certain you will enjoy. It is delicate and delicious too. If you are running late one evening, you will like the fact that this delightful dish can be assembled and cooked in less that fifteen minutes.

Veal Paprika in Cream

1 1/2 pounds veal scallops, cut into pieces, seasoned
    with salt, white pepper and garlic powder
2 tablespoons butter
1 onion, chopped fine
1/2 pound mushrooms, sliced
2 tablespoons flour
1/4 cup white wine
2 tablespoons paprika
2 teaspoons chicken seasoned stock base dissolved in
    1 cup water
1 cup cream
salt and pepper to taste

Saute scallops in butter for a few minutes, until they lose their pinkness. They are very tender, so do not overcook. Remove veal from skillet and set aside.

In same pan, add onions and saute until onions are soft.

Add mushrooms and saute another five minutes. Add a little more butter, if necessary. Add flour and cook for a minute or two. Add wine and cook and stir for another minute.

Add paprika, chicken stock and cook until heated through and sauce thickens. Add veal and cream. Taste for salt and pepper. Heat through. Serve with Buttered Noodles with Onions and Poppy Seeds. Serves 6.

Poultry & Dressings

My daughter, when she was 10 years old, received a little note from a boy in her class. It read, "I love you very much. That is why I am using my best handwriting." I am not entirely certain what it was about that note that made it so beautiful. I do know, that the classic simplicity touched upon a sentiment that we have all shared at one time or another.

When we use our "best handwriting" or wear our prettiest dress, or use our best china, or prepare our very best dish, we are saying, "I like you." in just another way.

Well, Chicken Breasts with Herbed Stuffing and Sour Cream Mushroom Sauce is one of my favorites. Chicken breasts, stuffed with a delectable dressing and lavished with a very special sour cream and wine sauce, is simply spectacular for formal dinners, but easy enough to be included in your repertoire. Serve it with a lovely pilaf and some spiced peaches and get ready for a standing ovation.

Chicken Breasts with Herbed Stuffing & Sour Cream Mushroom Sauce

4 chicken breasts (Ask butcher to remove the bones and gently flatten.) Sprinkle lightly with salt, white pepper, garlic powder and paprika.

2 cups fresh white bread, cubed, (about 6 slices). Remove crusts.
1/4 teaspoon paprika
1/4 teaspoon poultry seasoning
1/2 teaspoon salt
white pepper to taste
1/4 cup water
1 teaspoon chicken seasoned stock base
1 tablespoon finely chopped onion
3 tablespoons melted butter

CHICKEN BREASTS WITH HERB STUFFING (Cont.)

Mash all the ingredients together until they are thoroughly blended. Divide stuffing into 4 parts. Place 1 part stuffing in center of chicken breast, roll and secure with tooth picks. Roll stuffed breasts in flour.

In pan you will bake breasts, melt 4 tablespoons butter. Roll stuffed breasts in butter and bake at 325° for about 1 hour and 15 minutes. Baste with butter frequently during baking.

Serve with Sour Cream and Mushroom Sauce ladled on top. Decorate with parsley and whole spiced peaches. Serves 4.

SOUR CREAM MUSHROOM SAUCE:

1/4 cup finely minced onion
2 tablespoons butter
1/4 pound mushrooms, thinly sliced
1 tablespoon flour
1/2 cup light cream
1/2 cup sour cream
salt and white pepper to taste
1 tablespoon sauterne or sherry

Saute onions in butter until they are soft. Add mushrooms and continue sauteing until mushrooms are tender. Add flour and cook for a minute or two. Add cream and cook over low heat, stirring, until sauce thickens. Add sour cream, seasonings and wine and heat through. Do not boil. Serve warm.

Cherry Glazed Chicken Breasts Stuffed with Wild Rice

8 chicken breasts (Ask butcher to remove skin and bones and gently flatten.) Sprinkle lightly with salt, paprika and garlic powder. Pepper is optional.

Wild Rice Stuffing

Cherry Glaze

Place 1 part stuffing in center of each chicken breast. Roll and secure with tooth picks or skewers. Roll stuffed breasts lightly in flour. Melt 1/2 cup butter (1 stick) in pan you will cook breasts. Roll stuffed breasts in butter and bake in a 325° oven for 1 hour and 15 minutes. Baste with Cherry Glaze 2 or 3 times during the last 45 minutes of baking.

WILD RICE STUFFING

Cook 1 package Herb Seasoned Wild and Long Grain Rice according to directions on the package. When rice is cooked, add 1/2 cup toasted slivered almonds. Divide stuffing into 8 parts.

Cherry Glaze

1 cup black cherry preserves
1/3 cup frozen orange juice concentrate. Do not dilute.
1 teaspoon grated orange zest.

Combine all the ingredients and heat through.

Note:
Chicken breasts can be assembled in the morning and refrigerated until baking time.

I have not found it satisfactory to freeze.

Old Fashioned Stuffed Chicken Seasoned with Herbs & Butter

1 Roasting chicken (about 5 pounds)
1 package Herb Seasoned Stuffing Mix

1 onion, finely chopped
1/2 cup celery, finely chopped
1/4 cup butter (1/2 stick)

1/4 pound mushrooms, thinly sliced
1 egg, beaten
1 tablespoon dried parsley flakes or 3 tablespoons
   fresh
1 teaspoon chicken seasoned stock base
1 teaspoon poultry seasoning
salt and pepper to taste
chicken broth (You can use the canned broth.)

Place stuffing mix in a large bowl and set aside. Saute
onion and celery in butter until they are soft. Add
mushrooms and saute until mushrooms are tender.
Add vegetables to stuffing mix.

Add remaining ingredients using only enough chicken
broth to hold stuffing together. Set aside.

Baste entire chicken, inside and out with basting mixture. Place stuffing loosely into neck and body of
chicken. Pull neck skin over to back and skewer it
down. Skewer body opening with 2 or 3 poultry pins.
Lace strings around pins, back and forth. At the last
turn, bring the string under the legs and tie them together. Tuck wings under. Baste again. Roast in a
350° oven for about 2 hours, basting every 15 or 20
minutes. Remove from oven, cut string and remove
pins and string. Serve with hot biscuits and gravy.
Serves 6.

BASTING MIXTURE:

1/3 cup melted butter   1 clove garlic
1/2 teaspoon salt   1/4 teaspoon onion powder
1/8 teaspoon pepper   2 tablespoons white wine
1 teaspoon paprika

Place all the ingredients in a blender container and
blend until garlic is completely ground.

Southern Fried Chicken Epicurean

2 fryer chickens, cut into pieces. Sprinkle with salt
and pepper and dredge in flour.

2 eggs beaten
2 tablespoons water
2 tablespoons grated Parmesan cheese

1 cup bread crumbs
1/2 teaspoon garlic powder
1 tablespoon paprika
1/2 cup grated Parmesan cheese
salt and pepper to taste

Beat together the eggs, water and 2 tablespoons
grated Parmesan and set aside. Combine crumbs,
garlic powder, paprika, grated cheese and salt and
pepper and mix together.

Dip prepared chicken pieces into the egg mixture and
then into the crumb mixture and set them on waxed
paper.

In a large skillet, heat 1/2-inch of oil. When a drop of
water skitters around, start frying chicken pieces. Fry
and turn chicken pieces until golden brown on both
sides. Serve with biscuits and honey. Serves 6.

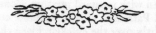

Chicken Teriyaki with Plum Glaze

2 fryer chickens, cut into pieces. Baste generously with Lawry's Teriyaki Marinade. Sprinkle with salt, pepper, garlic powder to taste.

Bake chicken in a preheated 325° oven for about 40 minutes. (Depending on size, chicken should be about half cooked.) Baste with Plum Glaze 2 or 3 times during the remainder of the cooking time, about 40 minutes more. Excellent with Fried Rice. Serves 6 to 8.

PLUM GLAZE

1 cup plum preserves
2 tablespoons ketchup
1 tablespoon vinegar
2 tablespoons brown sugar
pinch of ginger

Combine all the ingredients and heat through until well blended.

Chicken Francaise

2 frying chickens, cut into pieces, sprinkled with salt, pepper and garlic powder and dusted lightly with flour

1/4 cup butter (1/2 stick)
1/4 cup oil

In pan you will bake chicken, melt butter and mix in oil. Roll chicken pieces in butter, oil mixture and coat evenly. Bake chicken in a 325° oven for 45 minutes. Now baste with Francaise Sauce every 10 minutes until chicken is tender, about 30 minutes more. Serves 6.

FRANCAISE SAUCE

1 cup currant jelly
1 tablespoon lemon juice
1 teaspoon beef extract (or 1 teaspoon Beef Seasoned Stock Base)
2 tablespoons water

Combine all the ingredients and heat through until currant jelly is melted and mixture is well blended.

Chicken in Raisin & Currant Sauce

2 fryer chickens, cut into pieces. Sprinkle with salt,
   pepper, garlic powder and paprika.

1/2 cup butter

1/2 cup dry red wine
1/2 cup beef broth
1 cup golden raisins
1/2 cup currants
1/2 cup currant jelly
1/4 cup ketchup
1 package dry onion soup
salt and pepper to taste

Place prepared chicken in roasting pan and drizzle
with melted butter. Roast chicken in a 325° oven for
30 minutes, basting with butter 2 or 3 times.

Meanwhile, heat together the remaining ingredients
until the jelly is melted and the mixture is blended.
Pour this sauce evenly over the chicken and continue
baking for 45 minutes.

Serve with Sweet and Sour Red Cabbage and Potato
Pancakes.

Chicken A La King

3 cups diced cooked chicken

1/2 pound mushrooms, cleaned and sliced
2 tablespoons butter
1 jar (2 ounces) sliced pimentos
2 tablespoons flour
1 cup whipping cream
1 cup rich chicken broth
salt and white pepper to taste

Saute mushrooms in butter until they are tender.
Add pimentos and flour and cook for a minute or
two, stirring. Add cream and broth and seasonings
and cook stirring until sauce has thickened. Add
chicken and heat through. Serve with rice or on
patty shells. Serves 4.

Turkey Curry with Apples & Raisins

3 cups cooked turkey, cut into large dice

1 onion, finely chopped
1 clove garlic, pressed or mashed
4 tablespoons butter, 1/2 stick

2 tablespoons flour
2 teaspoons curry powder or to taste
salt and pepper to taste

1 apple, peeled, cored and grated
1 tablespoon brown sugar
1/2 cup golden raisins, plumped in oranged juice
1 cup turkey or chicken broth
1 cup sour cream

Saute onion and garlic in butter until onions are soft, but not brown. Add flour and cook and stir for a minute or so. Add curry powder, salt and pepper and mix well.

Add grated apple, brown sugar, raisins and broth. Cook over low heat, stirring until sauce thickens. (If the sauce is too thick, add a little more broth.) Taste and adjust seasonings. Add turkey and sour cream and heat through. Do not boil. Serves 6.

Note:
Entire dish can be made earlier in the day and refrigerated. Remove from the refrigerator about 1 hour before you are planning to heat it and let it come to room temperature. Reheat over low heat, stirring now and then, until heated through. Do not let the sauce boil.

Seasoned Salt for Poultry

This is one of my favorite combinations of herbs and spices. It is outstanding on chicken and turkey and makes the best tasting gravy.

1 1/2 cups salt
1 whole garlic, peeled
1 tablespoon poultry seasoning
1 tablespoon paprika
1/4 teaspoon ginger
1 teaspoon seasoned pepper
1/4 teaspoon powdered mustard
1 teaspoon chili powder
1 teaspoon toasted onion powder
1 1/2 teaspoons MSG

Place salt and garlic cloves in blender container and blend at high speed until garlic is thoroughly mashed. Remove salt and garlic mixture and place in a quart jar with a tight lid. Add the remaining ingredients and shake to thoroughly mix. Refrigerate. (Sprinkle over your buttered turkey or chicken as you would salt. Use a little less at first until you find the right amount for your taste.) Makes about 2 cups of heavenly seasoning.

Note:
Transfer some of the seasoned salt to a small shaker jar with large sprinkling holes. This makes it easier to use.

I like to store this seasoning in the refrigerator, but it isn't mandatory.

In a lovely amber glass jar, this seasoning makes an unforgettable gift from your kitchen.

Molds

Spiced Apricot Cream Mold

1 jar (1 pound 12 ounces) spiced apricots
water
1 package Jello, Orange (6 ounces)
1 carton Dsertwhip

Drain apricots and reserve the juice. Slice the apricots and remove the seeds. Set aside.

To the reserved juice, add water to make 2 1/2 cups liquid. Boil juice mixture with the orange gelatin until gelatin is dissolved. Cool gelatin until it is partially congealed, but not firm set.

Whip gelatin until it is light and frothy. Beat Dsertwhip until it is stiff like whipped cream. Combine whipped gelatin and whipped Dsertwhip until well mixed. (You can do this in your mixer, too.) Carefully add the sliced apricots. Pour mixture into a 2-quart mold and refrigerate until firm.

Unmold by placing mold into warm water for a few seconds until it is loosened and inverting it on a serving platter. Serves 12.

Note:
This is a spectacular mold and deserves your prettiest serving platter.

The apricots can be substituted with spiced peaches which is equally good.

Can be made the day before with excellent results. Unmold on the day you are planning to serve it.

Strawberry Mold with Sour Cream & Walnuts

1 package (6 ounces) strawberry gelatin
2 1/2 cups boiling water
1 package (10 ounces) frozen sliced strawberries in syrup, drained
1 pint sour cream
1/4 cup chopped, toasted walnuts

Add boiling water to strawberry gelatin and stir until it is dissolved. Add the juice of the drained strawberries. Cool the gelatin until it is partially congealed and not firm set. Beat gelatin until it is light and frothy. Add sour cream and continue beating until it is blended. Fold in the strawberries and the chopped walnuts.

Pour mixture into a 2-quart mold and refrigerate it until it is firm. When ready to serve, unmold and decorate with green leaves and fresh strawberries. Serves 12.

Note:
Sour cream will be beaten into small particles.

Strawberry, Blueberry & Banana Mold

1 package Jello, Strawberry, (6 ounces)
2 cups boiling water

1 package frozen strawberries in syrup (10 ounces)
1/2 cup frozen blueberries
1 banana, sliced thin

Combine gelatin and boiling water and stir until gelatin is dissolved. Add fruits and mix well. Pour mixture into a 2-quart mold and refrigerate until firm. Serve with a dollup of Creme Vanilla. Serves 8 to 10.

Apricot Orange Mold

1 large can apricots, 1 pound 12 ounces, drained
Boiling water and drained apricot juice

1 package Jello, Orange, 6 ounces

1 cup sour cream
1 cup vanilla ice cream

Drain apricots. Add water to drained apricot juice to total 2 cups liquid. Puree apricots in blender and set aside. (If apricots are whole, make certain you remove the seeds.) Boil water and juice mixture. Add gelatin and stir to dissolve.

Add the sour cream and ice cream and beat until thoroughly mixed. Add the pureed fruit and stir to mix well. Pour mixture into a 2-quart mold and refrigerate until firm.

Unmold by placing mold in warm water for a few seconds until it is loosened and inverting it on a serving platter. Serves 12.

Note:
Can be made and unmolded the day before. Decorate with orange slices and green leaves.

Orange Mold with Yogurt

1 package (6 ounces) orange gelatin
2 1/2 cups boiling water
1 cup unflavored yogurt
1 orange, grated. Remove any large pieces of membranes.
2 bananas, sliced

Add boiling water to orange gelatin and stir until it is dissolved. Add yogurt and stir until blended. Add orange and sliced bananas.

Pour mixture into a 2-quart mold and refrigerate it until it is firm. When ready to serve, unmold and decorate with orange slices and green leaves. Serves 10 or 12.

Cranberry Tangerine Mold

1 package Jello, Black Cherry, (6 ounces)
2 cups boiling water

1/2 can Cranberry Sauce, whole berry (use 8 ounce)
1 tangerine, grated, use fruit, peel and juice. Remove
   any large pieces of membranes
1 can crushed pineapple (1 pound 4 ounces)
1/2 cup toasted walnuts, chopped

Combine gelatin and boiling water. Stir until gelatin
is dissolved. Add the cranberry sauce and stir until
the sauce is melted and the berries float loosely. Add
remaining ingredients and stir to mix well. Pour mixture into a 2-quart mold and refrigerate until firm.
Unmold by placing mold in warm water for a few
seconds until it is loosened and inverting it on a serving platter.

Decorate mold with halved tangerine slices around
the rim and some pretty green leaves (that have been
rubbed, tubbed and scrubbed, of course.) Serves 12.

Raspberry, Banana & Sour Cream Mold

1 package Jello, Raspberry, 6 ounces
2 cups boiling water
1 cup sour cream
2 packages (10 ounces each) frozen raspberries in
   syrup, defrosted and sieved
2 bananas, sliced thin

Combine gelatin and boiling water. Stir until gelatin
is dissolved. Add the sour cream and beat until
smooth. You can use a hand mixer. Add the fruit and
mix well. Pour mixture into a 6-cup mold and refrigerate until firm. Unmold by placing mold in warm
water for a few seconds until it is loosened and inverting it on a serving platter. Decorate mold with a
ring of banana slices that were dipped in lemon juice.
Sprinkle with a few chopped walnuts.

Mandarin Orange Cream Cloud Mold

1 package (6 ounces) orange gelatin
2 1/2 cups boiling water

1 carton Dsertwhip (sweetened non-dairy whipping cream)
1 cup mandarin orange sections, drained

Add boiling water to orange gelatin and stir it until gelatin is dissolved. Cool gelatin until it is partially congealed and not firm set. Beat gelatin until it is light and frothy. Beat Dsertwhip until it is the consistency of whipped cream. On low setting of electric mixer, slowly beat together the gelatin and the whipped cream until the mixture is blended. Gently fold in drained mandarin orange sections.

Pour mixture into a 2-quart mold and refrigerate it until it is firm. When ready to serve, unmold and decorate it with orange slices and maraschino cherries. Serves 10 or 12.

Lime Mold with Mint & Creme

1 package (6 ounces) lime gelatin
2 1/2 cups boiling water
1 carton Dsertwhip (sweetened non-dairy whipping cream)
4 drops peppermint extract

Add boiling water to lime gelatin and stir until gelatin is dissolved. Cool gelatin until partially congealed and not firm set. Beat gelatin until it is light and frothy. Whip Dsertwhip until it is the consistency of whipped cream. On low setting of electric mixer, slowly beat together the gelatin and the whipped creme. Add a few drops of peppermint extract. (If the mixture appears pale, add a drop or two of green food coloring.) Pour mixture into a 2-quart mold and refrigerate until firm. When ready to serve, unmold and fill center with black grapes. Decorate with green leaves and serve with pride. Serves 12.

Noodles

&

Rice

The Best Noodle Pudding with Sour Cream & Raisins

8 ounces (1/2 pound) medium noodles, cooked and drained

1/2 cup butter (1 stick)

4 eggs
1 pint (2 cups) sour cream
1/2 cup milk
1 teaspoon vanilla
1 cup sugar
1/2 teaspoon salt

1 cup yellow raisins, soaked overnight in orange juice and drained
2 tablespoons cinnamon sugar

In a 9x13-inch pan, melt the butter. Add the cooked and drained noodles and toss them in the butter until they are completely coated.

Beat together the eggs, sour cream, milk, vanilla, sugar and salt until the mixture is well blended.

Pour the egg mixture over the noodles and spread noodles evenly in the pan. Sprinkle top with drained raisins and cinnamon sugar. Bake in a 350° oven for 1 hour. Cut into squares and serve warm. Serves 8.

Noodles with Sour Cream & Almonds

1/2 pound medium noodles, cooked and drained

3/4 stick butter (3 ounces), melted
1 cup sour cream
1/2 cup toasted slivered almonds

Cook noodles al dente (tender but still firm). Al dente literally means you can bite into them. Toss the noodles in the melted butter and then into the sour cream. Toss to coat evenly. Transfer noodles immediately to a serving dish, sprinkle with toasted almonds and serve hot. Serves 6.

Noodles with Poppy Seeds and Sour Cream

1 package (8 ounces) medium noodles, cooked and
  drained. Do not overcook.
1/2 cup onion, finely chopped
2 ounces butter (1/2 stick)
1 tablespoon poppy seeds
1 tablespoon lemon juice
1/2 cup sour cream
salt and pepper to taste

Saute onion in butter until onions are soft. In a large
bowl, combine all the ingredients and toss to mix
well. Place mixture into a lovely heat and serve casserole and heat in a 300° oven, covered, until hot.
Serves 6.

Parsleyed Noodles with Green Onions

1 package (8 ounces) medium noodles, cooked and
  drained
1/2 cup butter, (1 stick), melted
1/2 cup parsley, minced very fine (or 1/4 cup dry
  flakes)
2 tablespoons dried green onions
salt and pepper to taste

Combine all the ingredients and toss to mix well.
Serve immediately. Serves 6.

Note:
*You can make the noodles earlier in the day and re-
frigerate them before serving. In that case, place the
noodles in a lovely heat and serve casserole, sprinkle
with about 1 ounce of water, cover and reheat in a
300° oven until heated through.*

Noodle Souffle Milli

6 ounces medium noodles, cooked and drained

1/2 pound cream cheese
1/2 pound cottage cheese
1 cup sour cream
1/2 cup butter (1 stick)
1/2 cup sugar
1 teaspoon vanilla
6 eggs, separated

Ingredients should be at room temperature. Cream together the cream cheese, cottage cheese, sour cream and butter. Add sugar, vanilla and egg yolks, one at a time, beating well after each addition. Beat egg whites until they are stiff but not dry and fold them into the cheese mixture. Carefully fold in cooked noodles. Pour mixture into a buttered 9x13-inch pan and bake it in a 375° oven for about 45 minutes or until it is puffed and lightly browned. Serves 10.

Divine Noodle Pudding

3/4 pound broad noodles, cooked and drained
1/2 cup butter (1 stick)

5 eggs
8 ounces cream cheese, at room temperature
3/4 cup sugar, you can use 1 cup, if you like it sweeter
1/2 cup orange juice concentrate
1 1/2 cups milk

1 cup golden raisins, plumped in orange juice
2 teaspoons cinnamon sugar

In a 9x13-inch roasting pan, melt butter and toss the cooked noodles to coat evenly. In mixer, beat eggs with cream cheese until well blended. Add sugar, juice and milk and beat until smooth. Add raisins. Pour mixture over cooked noodles and spread evenly. Sprinkle top with cinnamon sugar. Bake in a 350° oven for about 1 hour. Serves 12.

Toasted Vermicelli with Toasted Almonds

8 ounces vermicelli coils
1 can (10 1/2 ounces) beef broth
1 cup water
2 tablespoons butter
salt and pepper to taste
1/2 cup toasted, slivered almonds

Toast vermicelli (also called fideos) in a 350° oven for about 8 minutes or until it is golden brown. Set aside.

Combine beef broth, water, butter and seasonings and bring mixture to a boil. Add toasted vermicelli, cover and reduce to low heat. Simmer mixture until vermicelli is tender and liquid is absorbed, about 10 minutes. Toss with toasted almonds before serving. Serves 6.

Fideos with Onions & Mushrooms

8 ounces fideo or vermicelli coils
2 tablespoons butter
1/2 onion, finely minced
1/4 pound mushrooms, finely chopped
2 tablespoons butter
2 1/2 cups rich chicken broth
salt and pepper to taste

Toast fideos in a 350° oven for about 8 minutes or until it is golden brown. Set aside.

Saute onion in 2 tablespoons butter until onion is soft. Add mushrooms and continue sauteing until mushrooms are tender. Set aside.

In a saucepan melt 2 tablespoons butter and add chicken broth, salt and pepper. Bring mixture to a boil and add toasted fideos. Lower heat and simmer until fideos are tender and liquid is absorbed, about 10 minutes. Add onion and mushroom mixture and toss to combine. Serves 6.

Fried Rice with Onions & Water Chestnuts

2 tablespoons butter
1 cup long grain rice
1 can (10 1/2 ounces) beef broth
1 cup water
1 tablespoon soy sauce
salt and pepper to taste

Saute rice in butter until rice is lightly browned. Add remaining ingredients and stir. Cover pan, lower heat and gently simmer rice until liquid is absorbed and rice is tender. When is rice is cooked, add:

6 strips bacon, crisped and crumbled
3 green onions, finely minced
6 water chestnuts, thinly sliced

Mix these into the rice and toss them to combine evenly. Heat through. Serves 6.

Mushroom Rice with Onions

1 small onion, finely chopped
3 tablespoons butter
1/4 pound sliced mushrooms
1 cup rice, long-grain

1 can (10 1/2 ounces) Campbell's Beef Broth
3/4 cup water
salt and pepper to taste
1/2 cup toasted slivered almonds

Saute onion in butter until onions are soft. Add mushrooms and continue cooking until mushrooms are tender. Add rice and cook and stir for about 5 minutes. Add a little more butter, if necessary.

In pan you will cook rice, heat broth, water, salt and pepper. Add rice and mushroom mixture and stir. Cover pan, lower heat and gently simmer rice until liquid is absorbed and rice is tender. Serve with toasted almonds sprinkled evenly over the top. Serves 5 or 6.

Yellow Rice with Tomatoes & Chiles

1 can (10 1/2 ounces) Campbell's Beef Broth
3/4 cup water
salt and pepper to taste
1/8 teaspoon tumeric
1 large tomato, skinned, seeded and chopped coarsely
1 tablespoon Ortega's Diced Green Chiles, or to taste
3 tablespoons butter
1 cup rice, long grain

Bring first seven ingredients to a boil in pan you will cook rice. Add rice, cover and reduce heat. Simmer rice slowly until liquid is absorbed and rice is tender. Serves 5 or 6.

Rice with Raisins & Almonds

2 1/3 cups water
3 teaspoons chicken seasoned stock base
1 cup long grain rice
2 tablespoons butter
salt, pepper and a pinch of garlic powder
1/2 teaspoon curry powder or to taste

Combine all the ingredients in a saucepan. Stir, cover and simmer over low heat until liquid is absorbed and rice is tender, about 30 minutes. When rice is cooked, add:

1 onion, sauteed in 2 tablespoons butter until golden
1/2 cup golden raisins, plumped in orange juice
1/2 cup slivered toasted almonds

Mix these well into the rice and heat through if necessary. Garnish with finely minced green onions. Serves 6.

Tomato Rice & Onions

1 onion, finely minced
2 tablespoons butter
1 cup long-grain rice
1 can (10 1/2 ounces) chicken broth
3/4 cup water
3 tablespoons tomato sauce
salt and pepper to taste

Saute onion in butter until onion is soft. Add remaining ingredients and bring to boil. Lower heat, cover and gently simmer rice until it is tender and liquid is absorbed. Serves 6.

Toasted Barley Casserole with Onions

1 cup toasted egg barley
1 package onion soup mix
2 3/4 cups water
2 tablespoons oil
salt and pepper to taste

Place all the ingredients in an ovenproof casserole. Stir and cover. Bake in a 350° oven until liquid is absorbed and barley is tender, about 1 hour. Serves 4 to 6.

Note:
You can add 1/2 pound sliced mushrooms that were sauteed in the butter for a delicious optional. Add the mushrooms after the barley is cooked.

Vegetables

If I were a poet, I would write a sonnet on the virtues of the vegetable. Perhaps no other food has created more wrinkled noses ... perhaps no other food has been more grumbled and rumbled and ended up tumbled than the poor, unsung vegetable.

Vegetables are not only "good for you", but they can really be good too. Because they are relatively low in carlories, you can splurge a little with butters and cream and an infinite variety of sauces.

Actually, vegetables can add a great deal of excitement to a meal. They need not be the silent accompaniments in the shadow of the main course, but so delicious that they can stand alone quite well.

Asparagus in Sour Cream Lemon Sauce with Garlic Crumbs

1 can (1 pound) asparagus spears, drained
1/2 cup sour cream
1/4 cup mayonnaise
1 1/2 tablespoons lemon juice, freshly squeezed
1/2 teaspoon grated lemon peel
salt to taste

1/2 cup garlic croutons, rolled into coarse crumbs

Lay drained asparagus in a heat and serve baker. Combine remaining ingredients, except the croutons, and spoon mixture over the asparagus. Sprinkle top with garlic crumbs. Heat in a 350° oven, until heated through. Brown under the broiler until golden, about 1 minute. Serves 4.

Note:
Entire dish can be assembled and refrigerated earlier in the day, except for sprinkling the crumbs, which I would do just before heating.

Asparagus in Lemon Cream Sauce

1 can asparagus spears *or*
1 package (10 ounces) frozen asparagus spears cooked
   according to the directions on the package
1 tablespoon melted butter
salt and pepper to taste

3/4 cup sour cream
1 tablespoon chopped chives
1 tablespoon lemon juice

1/2 cup toasted slivered almonds
1/2 cup Ritz Cracker crumbs or Waverly Cracker
   crumbs

Arrange cooked asparagus in a baking dish. Drizzle
with melted butter and sprinkle lightly with salt and
pepper.

In a small bowl, mix together the sour cream, chopped chives and lemon juice. Spread sour cream mixture
evenly over the asparagus.

Sprinkle with slivered almonds and cracker crumbs.
Heat through in a 325° oven. Do not overcook. Then
broil for a few seconds to brown the crumbs. Serves 4.

Asparagus in Cream Cheese Hollandaise

2 packages (3 ounces, each) cream cheese
2 tablespoons cream
3 egg yolks
1 1/2 tablespoons lemon juice
1/2 teaspoon finely grated lemon peel
pinch of salt and white pepper

2 packages (10 ounces, each) frozen asparagus,
   cooked firm

Beat all the ingredients together, except the asparagus, until they are blended. Place mixture on the top
of a double boiler over hot water. Cook, stirring until
heated through. Spoon warm sauce over hot asparagus and broil until lightly colored. Serves 8.

Broccoli with Lemon Cream

2 packages frozen broccoli, 10 ounces each, defrosted
6 eggs
3/4 cup half and half
3/4 cup mayonnaise
2 tablespoons lemon juice
salt and pepper to taste

Place broccoli in a buttered baking dish in one layer. Beat eggs with cream and mayonnaise until well blended. Add lemon juice, salt and pepper. Pour mixture over the broccoli.

Bake in a 350° oven for about 30 minutes. Sprinkle top of casserole with Ritz Parmesan Topping and continue baking for another 15 minutes or until crumbs are golden. Serves 4 for lunch.

RITZ PARMESAN TOPPING

1/4 cup Ritz cracker crumbs
1/4 cup Parmesan cheese

Combine crumbs and cheese and toss to blend evenly.

Broccoli with Hollandaise Sauce

3 egg yolks
1 1/2 tablespoons lemon juice
pinch of salt and white pepper
3/4 cup butter (1 1/2 sticks)

2 packages, (10 ounces, each) frozen broccoli, cooked firm

Place the egg yolks, lemon juice, salt and pepper in the blender container. Blend for 10 seconds at high speed.

Heat butter until it is sizzling hot and bubbly, but be careful not to brown it. Add the hot, sizzling butter very slowly, in a steady stream, while the blender continues running at high speed. When the butter is completely incorporated, sauce is ready. Spoon warm sauce over hot broccoli. Serve at once. Serves 8.

Sweet & Sour Red Cabbage with Apples & Raisins

1 jar (1 pound) red cabbage (sweet and sour)
1 apple, peeled, cored and grated
1/4 cup golden raisins
3 tablespoons lemon juice
salt to taste

Combine all the ingredients and cook over low heat until apples are tender, about 15 minutes. So good and traditionally served with Sauerbraten and dumplings. Serves 4 or 5.

Carrots with Apples and Raisins

1 package frozen baby carrots (whole), 10 ounces

2 tablespoons butter
2 tablespoons brown sugar
1 teaspoon lemon juice
1/2 cup golden raisins, plumped overnight in orange juice
1 apple, peeled and grated
1 tablespoon finely minced parsley
salt and pepper to taste

Cook carrots in salted water until they are tender and drain. In a skillet, melt the butter and add the brown sugar. Stir to mix. Add all the ingredients and continue cooking and stirring until apples are tender and carrots are glazed. Serves 4 or 5.

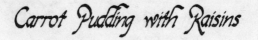

Carrot Pudding with Raisins

1 can (1 pound) julienned carrots (or sometimes called Carrots French Style) drained and dried on paper towelling

1/2 cup sweet butter
1/2 cup brown sugar
1/4 cup sugar
2 eggs
1 tablespoon lemon juice

1 cup flour
1 teaspoon baking powder
1/2 teaspoon baking soda
1/4 teaspoon salt

1 teaspoon vanilla
1/2 cup yellow raisins, plumped in orange juice

Drain carrots and pat them dry with paper towelling. Beat together the butter, sugar, eggs and lemon juice until the mixture is smooth, about 2 minutes. Add dry ingredients and beat until blended, about 1 minute. Add vanilla and yellow raisins and beat until blended. Stir in the carrots.

Place mixture in a heavily greased and floured 2-quart ring mold. Bake at 350° for about 50 minutes or until a cake tester inserted in center comes out clean. Remove from the oven, loosen edges and carefully invert onto a serving platter. Fill center with whole berry cranberry sauce. Serve with turkey or chicken. Serves 8 to 10.

Green Beans with French Fried Onions

2 packages (10 ounces each) frozen French style green beans, defrosted

1 tablespoon butter
2 teaspoons beef seasoned stock base
2 tablespoons water
1 jar (4 ounces) sliced mushrooms, drained

salt and pepper to taste
1 can (3 ounces) Durkee/O&C Real French Fried Onions

In a 12-inch skillet cook together the green beans, butter, stock base, water and mushrooms over low heat until the green beans are almost tender. Season with salt and pepper. Place mixture in a shallow baker and sprinkle top with French Fried Onions. Cover and refrigerate. Heat in a 300° oven until heated through. Serves 4 or 5.

Note:
If you are planning to cook-and-serve this dish, then sprinkle top with the French Fried Onions before you cook the green beans.

Instant Oven-Fried Eggplant

1 eggplant, peeled and sliced into 3/8-inch slices
mayonnaise

20 Ritz crackers, rolled into crumbs
1 cup grated Parmesan cheese

Spread each slice of eggplant on both sides with mayonnaise. Dip each slice into mixture of crumbs and grated cheese so that they are well coated on both sides.

Place eggplant slices on a greased cookie sheet and bake at 400° until golden brown, about 20 minutes. Carefully turn and brown other side. Serves 5 or 6.

Green Peas with Onions & Mushrooms

1 package (10 ounces) frozen peas, defrosted
1/2 onion, finely chopped
1/4 cup butter (1/2 stick)
1/4 pound mushrooms, cleaned and sliced
4 slices bacon, cooked crisp and crumbled
1 teaspoon chicken seasoned stock base
salt and pepper to taste

3/4 cup sour cream

Defrost peas. Saute onion in butter until onion is transparent. Add mushrooms and saute until mushrooms are tender. Add peas, bacon, stock base, salt and pepper, cover and cook until peas are almost tender. Add sour cream and mix through. If you are planning to serve it at once, heat and serve. If not, place mixture in a heat and serve casserole and refrigerate it. Heat through just before serving. Serves 4 to 6.

Creamed Potatoes with Bacon & Onions

6 large potatoes, peeled and sliced
2 medium onions, slice in rings
3 tablespoons butter
6 slices bacon, crisped and crumbled
1 can (10 1/2 ounces) beef broth
1 cup cream
salt and freshly ground pepper

Saute onions in butter until onions are soft. In an oven proof casserole layer the potatoes and onions. Combine the remaining ingredients and pour into the casserole. Bake in a 350° oven, covered, about 1 hour or until potatoes are tender. Serves 6.

Potatoes Baked in Butter

This is one of my absolute favorite and easiest method of preparing potatoes. Like a faithful friend, they are consistently good.

6 potatoes, medium-sized, peeled
salt to taste
4 tablespoons butter, 1/2 stick, melted

Melt the butter in the pan you will bake the potatoes. Brush the peeled potatoes with the melted butter, being careful to cover the entire potato. Bake uncovered in a 350° oven, basting and turning every 15 minutes until potatoes are tender and outside is golden and crusty. Keep warm in a low oven until ready to serve. (Can be held for at least 1/2 hour.)

Potatoes with Onions & Mushrooms

6 potatoes, medium sized, peeled

1 large onion, finely chopped
6 tablespoons butter, (3/4 stick)
1/2 pound mushrooms, sliced
salt and pepper to taste
1/2 cup cream

Boil potatoes in salted water until barely tender. Do not overcook. Slice potatoes crosswise into 1/2-inch thick slices. Set aside.

Saute onions in butter until onions are soft. Add mushrooms and continue sauteing until mushrooms are tender. Add cream and seasonings and stir to mix. Place sliced potatoes in a shallow casserole and spread onion mixture evenly over the top. Bake in a 350° oven for about 20 minutes or until piping hot. Serves 6.

Potato & Onion Cake
with Sour Cream & Apple Sauce

6 potatoes, peeled and grated
3 small onions, grated

2 eggs, beaten
1/2 cup cracker meal
pinch of garlic powder
salt and pepper to taste

3 tablespoons salad oil
1 tablespoon salad oil

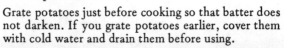

Grate potatoes just before cooking so that batter does not darken. If you grate potatoes earlier, cover them with cold water and drain them before using.

Combine onions, eggs, meal and seasonings. Add grated potatoes to onion mixture. Preheat oven to 350°. Place 3 tablespoons oil in a 9x13-inch baking pan and heat the pan in the oven. Add potato mixture to preheated pan and spread evenly. Drizzle 1 tablespoon oil over the top.

Return pan to the oven and cook until potatoes are tender and crust is a golden brown, about 45 minutes to 1 hour. Slice to serve. Serve with sour cream or Orange Apple Sauce. Serves 8.

Note:
You might enjoy serving this as an hors d'oeuvre. Slice into 1-inch squares and serve with bowls of sour cream and apple sauce.

Can be cooked earlier in the day and reheated at time of serving.

Do not freeze.

Potato Pancakes
with Orange Apple Sauce ---
Made in your Blender

2 eggs
1/4 cup cream
2 heaping tablespoons flour
3/4 teaspoon salt
1/2 teaspoon baking powder
pepper to taste

2 cups potatoes, peeled and cubed
1 onion, sliced

Place first six ingredients in a blender container. Blend for 10 seconds. Add potatoes and onion and blend for another 10 seconds or until potatoes and onions are cut into small particles but not smooth. Do not overblend.

Heat a 12-inch skillet with 1/2-inch oil. When a drop of water skitters around start making the pancakes. Pour 1/4 cup batter for each pancake but do not crowd them in the pan. Fry until golden brown on one side; turn and brown other side. Keep warm in a low oven. Serve warm with Orange Apple Sauce. Serves 6.

Orange Apple Sauce

1 jar (1 pound) applesauce
3 ounces (1/2 can) frozen orange juice concentrate, defrosted

Combine the applesauce and orange juice concentrate and mix until blended.

Potatoes Stuffed with Bacon & Chives

4 large baking potatoes, rubbed, tubbed and scrubbed

4 tablespoons butter
1/2 cup grated Parmesan cheese
1 tablespoon dried chopped chives
1 tablespoon dried parsley flakes
4 strips bacon, crisped and crumbled
salt and pepper to taste

cream as needed
paprika

Bake potatoes in a 400° oven until cooked through. Slice 1/2-inch off the tops and scoop out the potatoes carefully to keep the skins intact. Mash the potatoes while they are still hot. Add butter, grated cheese, chopped chives, parsley, bacon and lots of salt and pepper and mix until blended. Add a little cream to make it smooth.

Spoon potatoes back into their shells. Sprinkle with paprika, cover and refrigerate. Heat through in a 350° oven before serving. Serves 4.

Note:
These potatoes freeze beautifully. Simply defrost, heat through and serve.

Paprika Parsleyed Potatoes

1 can boiled sliced potatoes, drained (1 pound)
1/4 cup butter, (1/2 stick) melted
1/2 teaspoon paprika
1 teaspoon dried parsley flakes
1 teaspoon dried onion flakes
salt and pepper to taste

In a skillet, combine all the ingredients. Gently saute potatoes until lightly crisped. Serves 4.

Instant Creamed Spinach

1 package frozen spinach (10 ounces)
1 package cream cheese with chives (3 ounces)
dash of nutmeg
salt and pepper to taste

Combine all the ingredients and heat over a low flame until mixture is hot and cream cheese has melted. Serves 4.

Creamed Spinach with Bacon & Mushrooms

2 packages (10 ounces, each) frozen chopped spinach, defrosted

1/2 pound cream cheese, room temperature
6 slices bacon, fried crisp and crumbled
1 jar (4 ounces) sliced mushrooms, drained dry
salt and pepper to taste

Combine all the ingredients and cook over low heat until mixture is hot and cream cheese is melted. Serves 8.

Onions Carmelized in Brown Sugar

4 large onions, cut in half and thinly sliced
4 tablespoons butter
1/4 teaspoon paprika
2 tablespoons brown sugar
salt and pepper to taste

Saute onions in butter until they are transparent. Add remaining ingredients and continue sauteing until onions are glazed and golden brown. Serve with steak, London broil, hamburgers.

Zucchini, Chile, Tomato Casserole

1 onion, thinly sliced
1 tablespoon butter
1 1/2 pounds zucchini, peeled and sliced on the diagonal
1 teaspoon chicken seasoned stock base
2 tomatoes, cut into medium slices
1 can, 4-ounces, diced green chiles
salt and pepper to taste

1 cup sour cream
1 cup grated Jack cheese

Saute onion in butter until onion is tender. Add zucchini and continue sauteing until zucchini are cooked but still firm. Add a little more butter as necessary. Sprinkle zucchini with chicken seasoned stock base, salt and pepper.

In an 8x12-inch pyrex baking dish, layer the zucchini-onion mixture, tomatoes and chiles. Cover vegetables evenly with the sour cream and sprinkle top with the Jack cheese.

Bake in a 350° oven until heated through and cheese is melted and bubbly, about 20 or 25 minutes. Serves 6.

Note:
Casserole can be cooked ahead up to the point of adding the layer of sour cream and Jack cheese. Do this at the time you are planning to reheat the casserole.

Desserts

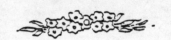

When I stop and think of what Adam and Eve risked for a simple dessert like an apple, I shudder to imagine what they would have chanced for an elegant dessert like a Tarte Tartin. Eve would blanch with shame if she could contemplate her lack of creativity.

Of course you know I love desserts. Whether they are light and refreshing or rich and exciting, for me, no dinner is complete without dessert.

The grand finale is, in a sense, a high point of dinner as well, for, when you really think about it, more time is spent lingering over dessert and coffee than any other course of the meal. Moreover, dessert is the only course that truly stands alone.

So, if you are planning an excellent finale to dinner or if you are inviting friends for a grand dessert and coffee, I hope you enjoy some of the following. Some are simple, some extravagant. Some can be prepared literally in minutes and some take a little longer . . . but are well worth the extra effort.

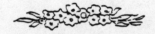

Chocolate Torte Darling
(Made in your Blender)

Don't be misled by the simplicity of this recipe. It produces one of the finest tasting tortes. It takes minutes to assemble, can be made ahead and not the least of its virtues, it freezes beautifully. This recipe makes 1 layer.

4 eggs, extra large
3/4 cups sugar
1 cup walnuts or pecans
1 teaspoon vanilla
2 tablespoons flour
2 1/2 teaspoons baking powder
2 tablespoons cocoa

Place eggs in blender container and whip for a few seconds. Add the remaining ingredients, in the order listed, and blend at high speed for 1 full minute.

Pour batter into a 10-inch layer pan with a removable bottom that has been greased and lightly dusted with flour. Repeat this for the second layer. Bake at 350° for about 20 minutes or until a cake tester inserted in center comes out clean. (You can bake the two layers at one time.) Fill and frost with Chocolate Whipped Cream.

Chocolate Whipped Cream

Beat 1 1/2 cups whipping cream with 3/4 cup Hershey's Chocolate Syrup until cream is thick and of spreading consistency.

Note:
You can make a single layer with equally good results. However, in that case, bake the single layer in a 9-inch pie pan or 9-inch square pan. Frost with only 3/4 cup of whipping cream.

Darling Carrot Cake

4 eggs
1 1/2 cups Crisco oil
1/2 pound cream cheese
1 teaspoon vanilla

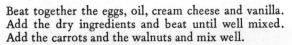

2 cups flour
2 cups sugar
2 teaspoons baking powder
1 teaspoon baking soda
1/2 teaspoon salt
2 teaspoons cinnamon

1 cup chopped walnuts
3 cups grated carrots

Beat together the eggs, oil, cream cheese and vanilla.
Add the dry ingredients and beat until well mixed.
Add the carrots and the walnuts and mix well.

Pour batter into a greased and floured 9x13-inch pan
or into *two* 9-inch angel pans. Bake in a 350° oven
for about 40-45 minutes for the 9x13-inch pan and
for about 35-40 minutes for the 2 angel pans. In
either case, test for doneness . . . when a cake tester
inserted in center comes out clean. Cool and frost
with Cream Cheese Frosting.

Cream Cheese Frosting

1/2 cup (1 stick) butter
1/2 pound cream cheese
1 teaspoon vanilla
1 pound sifted powdered sugar

Beat butter and cream cheese together until well
blended. Add vanilla and sugar and beat until smooth.
Will frost *two* 9-inch round cakes. (If you are making
a 9x13-inch cake, prepare only 1/2 the recipe.)

Note:
*This cake freezes beautifully, with or without the
frosting. Therefore, I would recommend your preparing the 2 angel pans. Use one and freeze the other.*

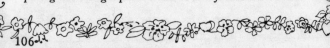

Velvet Cheesecake with Strawberry Orange Syrup

Crust: 1 1/2 cups graham cracker crumbs
3 ounces butter, (3/4 stick), softened
1/2 cup coarsely chopped walnuts
4 tablespoons cinnamon sugar

Filling: 1 pound cream cheese
1 cup sugar
3 eggs
3 cups sour cream
2 teaspoons vanilla
1 teaspoon almond extract or orange zest
2 tablespoons undiluted frozen orange juice, defrosted

Combine the crumbs, butter, walnuts and sugar and mix well until blended. With your fingers, press mixture on the bottom and 1-inch up the sides of a 9-inch springform pan.

In your electric mixer bowl, beat together the cream cheese, sugar, eggs, sour cream, vanilla, almond extract (or orange zest) and concentrated orange juice until mixture is smooth and blended. Pour mixture into the prepared crust.

Bake in a 350° oven for about 50 minutes or until a cake tester inserted in center comes out clean, no longer. Do not overbake. Cool in pan and then refrigerate for at least 4 to 6 hours. Overnight is better. Remove from pan and serve with a spoonful of Strawberry Orange Syrup. Serves 10.

Strawberry Orange Syrup

1 package frozen strawberries in heavy syrup, (10 ounces) defrosted
3 ounces (1/2 can) frozen orange juice, undiluted
1 tablespoon finely grated orange peel

Combine all the ingredients and refrigerate until serving.

Royal Cake Darling

I call this cake "royal" because it is literally fit to serve a "king". It is glorious in taste and texture. The combination of walnuts and apricots and whipped cream, you have probably guessed, makes it one of my very, very favorites. And not the least of its virtues is that it can be prepared in your blender ... in literally minutes. This recipe makes 1 layer. You must repeat the recipe for the second layer.

4 eggs
1 cup shelled walnuts or pecans
3/4 cup sugar
1 teaspoon vanilla
2 tablespoons flour
2 teaspoons baking powder

3/4 cup apricot jam, sieved

Place eggs in blender container and whip at high speed for a few seconds. Add the walnuts, sugar, vanilla, flour and baking powder and blend at high speed for 1 minute. Batter will be smooth. Pour the batter into a 10-inch layer pan with a removable bottom, that has been greased and lightly floured. Repeat for second layer. Bake immediately in a preheated oven at 350° for about 20-25 minutes or until a cake tester inserted in center comes out clean. You can bake the two layers at the same time.

Remove from oven, remove rings and allow layers to cool on metal bottoms. When completely cool, remove the first layer carefully (use a sharp knife) and place on your prettiest footed cake plate. Spread apricot jam over the first layer. Top with second layer and frost top and sides of cake with whipped cream. (Reserve about 1 cup.) Place reserved whipped cream in a pastry bag and decorate top of cake. Decorate with dots of apricot jam. Refrigerate overnight. Serves 12.

Chocolate Chip Sour Cream Cake

1 package (18 1/2 ounces) yellow cake mix
3/4 cup water
1 cup sour cream
2 eggs
1 cup chocolate chips, semi-sweet, coarsely crushed

3 tablespoons chocolate flavored Nestle's Quik

In your electric mixer, beat together the cake mix, water, sour cream and eggs. Beat at medium speed for 4 minutes. Add chocolate chips and mix until blended.

Place half the batter in a greased and floured 9-inch angel pan. Sprinkle the chocolate powder evenly over the batter. Pour the remaining batter evenly over the chocolate powder. With your scraper, cut into the batter at 2-inch intervals.

Bake in a 325° oven for about 50 minutes or until a cake tester inserted in center comes out clean. Dust lightly with sifted powdered sugar when cool.

Chocolate Chip Chocolate Cake

1 package (18 1/2 ounces) chocolate cake mix
1 cup sour cream
4 eggs
1/2 cup oil
1 package (3 3/4 ounces) instant chocolate pudding

1 cup chocolate chips, semi-sweet, coarsely crushed

In your electric mixer beat together all the ingredients except the chocolate chips. Beat mixture for 3 minutes at medium speed. Add the chocolate chips and beat for another minute.

Place batter in a buttered and floured 9-inch angel pan. Bake in a 325° oven for about 50 minutes or until a cake tester inserted in center comes out clean. Cool cake in pan. Dust lightly with sifted powdered sugar when cool.

If you don't tell, no one will ever guess . . . and when you tell, no one will hardly believe, that this absolutely divine and heavenly angel cake took less than 5 minutes to assemble. This angel dessert is really heaven sent, for it is elegant enough for a formal dinner, so delicious for children and grown-ups as well, and yet so simple you can truly depend on it when you are pressed for time.

As if all that were not enough, it also freezes exceptionally well and without any loss of flavor or texture. No temperamental primadonna, it can even be made a day ahead and stored in the refrigerator with absolute confidence that there will be no alteration of taste.

This recipe will fill and frost 2 7-inch angel cakes. Use one and freeze the other.

And then, when friends drop in and you tell them it is a little something you whipped up in five minutes, they will hardly believe you . . . until you tell.

Heavenly Angel Cake with Chocolate Cream

2 7-inch prepared angel cakes (from the bakery section in your market)

1 can (1 pound 1/2 ounce) Betty Crocker's Ready to Spread Chocolate Frosting

1 recipe Light Chocolate Whipped Cream

Cherries or grated chocolate to decorate

This recipe will fill and frost 2 angel cakes. Use one and freeze the other.

Cut angel cakes into 3 even layers, each. Starting with the bottom layer, cover with chocolate frosting and then with chocolate whipped cream. Repeat this for the second and third layer. Cover entire cake, tops and sides with Chocolate Whipped Cream. Decorate with grated chocolate and/or Maraschino cherries. Each cake serves 6.

Light Chocolate Whipped Cream

1 pint whipping cream
6 ounces Hershey's Chocolate Syrup
1 tablespoon Creme de Cacao Liqueur

Whip the cream until it is light and fluffy. Slowly add the chocolate syrup while continuing beating. Add liqueur and beat until stiff. Will frost 2 7-inch angel cakes.

Pumpkin Orange Cake with Orange Glaze

1 package (18 1/2 ounces) yellow cake mix
2 teaspoons pumpkin pie spice
2 teaspoons baking soda
1 1/2 cups canned pumpkin
2 eggs
1/4 cup orange juice
1 teaspoon orange peel
1 cup chopped walnuts
1 cup golden raisins, plumped overnight in orange juice and drained

In you mixer bowl, place cake mix, pumpkin pie spice, baking soda, pumpkin, eggs, orange juice, orange peel, and beat for 3 minutes at medium speed. Stir in the walnuts and raisins. Pour batter into a greased and lightly floured 9-inch angel pan. Bake at 350° for 40 to 45 minutes or until a cake tester inserted in center comes out clean. Cool cake in a pan. Turn cake out on a lovely platter and drizzle with orange glaze. Serves 10.

Orange Glaze

1 cup powdered sugar, sifted
2 tablespoons orange juice
1/2 teaspoon orange extract

Combine orange juice and extract. Add only enough powdered sugar to make glaze thick, yet still able to run off the spoon. Swirl on cake and drip down the sides.

Note:
You can substitute the raisins with 1 package (6 ounces) semi-sweet chocolate chips. The cake takes on a totally different character but is equally delicious.

Spiced Applesauce Cake

1/2 cup butter
1 cup sugar
1 egg
1/4 cup sour cream

1 1/2 cups cake flour, sifted
1 teaspoon baking soda
1 teaspoon baking powder
1 1/2 teaspoons pumpkin pie spice
pinch of salt
1 cup applesauce

1/4 cup cake flour
1/2 cup golden raisins
1/2 cup currants
1 cup chopped walnuts

Cream butter with sugar until light and fluffy. Add egg and beat well. Add sour cream and continue beating.

Combine dry ingredients, flour, soda, baking powder, pumpkin pie spice and salt. Add dry ingredients and applesauce alternately to creamed mixture, beating well after each addition.

Dredge raisins, currants and walnuts in 1/4 cup flour and add these to the batter.

Bake in a well-greased 10-inch tube pan for about 45 or 50 minutes or until a cake tester inserted in center comes out clean. Cool before removing from the pan. Drizzle Orange Glaze over the top. Serves 10 or 12.

Orange Glaze

3 tablespoons orange juice
1 1/2 cups sifted powdered sugar

Combine orange juice with only enough sugar to thicken it. Drizzle glaze over the cake and let it run down the sides.

Swiss Butter Crescents

This delightful cookie recipe was given to me by a friend's Swiss cook who was an extraordinary baker. Her directions were to "put your hand in the sugar bag and take out 1 handful of sugar." I followed her instructions and came up with the 3 heaping tablespoons of sugar. It worked fine.

1/2 cup butter, 1 stick
3 heaping tablespoons sifted powdered sugar
1/2 cup very finely chopped walnuts
1 cup flour, sifted

Cream butter and sugar together. Add flour and work into a smooth dough with your fingers. Add nuts and blend well.

Shape 1/2 teaspoonful of dough into tiny crescents. Place on a lightly greased cookie sheet and bake at 350° until light golden. Do not let them brown. They should be pale and delicate. When cool, sprinkle heavily with sifted Vanilla Sugar or powdered sugar. Makes about 40 cookies.

Butter Pecan Balls

1/2 pound butter, 2 sticks
1/2 cup sugar
2 teaspoons vanilla
2 cups finely chopped pecans
2 cups cake flour
sifted powdered sugar

Cream butter with sugar. Add vanilla, nuts and flour and mix thoroughly until blended. Shape into 3/4-inch balls. Bake at 300° on a lightly greased cookie sheet for about 25-30 minutes. Roll in powdered sugar when hot and again when cold. Makes about 60 cookies.

Note:
These cookies freeze beautifully. Simply roll them in sifted powdered sugar after defrosting.

Raspberry Button Cookies

This recipe was given to me 20 years ago by a dear friend. It is still one of my favorites.

1/2 cup butter (1 stick)
1/4 cup brown sugar
1 egg yolk
1 cup flour
1/2 teaspoon vanilla
1/2 cup finely chopped walnuts
1 egg white, beaten slightly
Raspberry jam, sieved

Cream butter and sugar together. Add egg yolk and blend well. Add vanilla and beat for about 1 minute. Add flour and work it into a smooth dough. Refrigerate dough for 1 hour.

Shape dough into 1/2-inch balls, dip into egg white and then into the chopped nuts. Place on a greased cookie sheet. Make an impression in the center of each cookie with your thumb or index finger.

Bake at 325° about 25 minutes. Press center down again, if they have puffed up. Fill center with 1/2 teaspoon raspberry jam when cool.

Note:
Cookies can be frozen with or without the jelly centers. However, I would recommend filling the jelly centers after defrosting.

You can substitute your favorite jelly or jam for the raspberry jam.

Chocolate Chip Chewies

1 can, 14 ounces, condensed milk
1 package, 6 ounces, milk chocolate chips
1/2 cup chopped walnuts
1 1/2 cups graham cracker crumbs

Combine all the ingredients and mix together until they are well blended. Heavily grease a pan measuring 6x12x1 inches. Place batter in pan and spread evenly. Bake in a preheated 350° oven for about 30 minutes. Cool for 5 minutes and cut into 1½ inch squares. Remove from pan immediately and cool on a brown paper bag. When cool, dust generously with sifted powdered sugar. Makes 32 chewies, 1 1/2-inches each.

Pecan Cherry Bar Cookies

1/2 cup butter, 1 stick, softened
1/4 cup vegetable shortening
1 egg yolk
3/4 cup sugar
1 3/4 cups flour, sifted
1 teaspoon vanilla

1 lightly beaten egg white
1 cup chopped pecans
3 tablespoons finely chopped maraschino cherries

In a bowl combine butter, shortening, egg yolk, sugar, flour and vanilla. Knead mixture gently with your fingers until the dough is smooth. Pat dough evenly with your fingers on a buttered cookie sheet. Brush top lightly with beaten egg white. Sprinkle top with chopped pecans and chopped cherries. Pat nuts and cherries gently into the dough. Bake in a 350° oven until golden brown, about 25 minutes. Remove from the oven and cut into squares or diamonds while still warm. Remove from cookie sheet and cool on a rack or a brown paper bag.

Mother's Lemon Cloud Cookies

1/2 cup butter
1 cup flour
1/4 cup powdered sugar

2 eggs
1 cup sugar
2 tablespoons flour
1/2 teaspoon baking powder
Grated rind of 1 lemon
2 1/2 tablespoons lemon juice

Beat butter, flour and sugar together until blended. Pat mixture into a lightly buttered 9x9-inch pan. Bake for 15 minutes in a 350° oven. While it is baking, beat the eggs and the sugar together. Add remaining ingredients and beat until blended.

Pour this mixture on the baked crust. Bake for an additional 25 minutes. Allow to cool. Cut into squares and sprinkle with sifted powdered sugar.

No-Bake Brownies

4 cups vanilla wafer crumbs
1 cup walnuts
1/2 cup sifted powdered sugar
3/4 cup evaporated milk
1 package (12 ounces) semi-sweet chocolate chips
1 teaspoon vanilla

Combine crumbs, walnuts and sugar. Heat evaporated milk. Add chocolate and stir until chocolate is melted. Add vanilla. Combine chocolate and crumb mixtures and mix well. Press into a 9x9-inch pan and refrigerate overnight. Cut into 1 1/2-inch squares. Makes 36 brownies.

Chocolate Iced Cream

This is a delightful, light and very delicious iced cream. It does away with laborious methods of beating, freezing and beating again.

6 egg whites, beaten with a pinch of salt
8 tablespoons sugar

2 cups heavy whipping cream
3/4 cup Hershey's Chocolate Syrup
2 tablespoons Creme de Cacao

1/2 pound sweet or semi-sweet chocolate, melted over hot, not boiling water

In your electric mixer, beat egg whites with a pinch of salt until soft peaks form. Add sugar slowly and continue beating until a stiff meringue. Set aside. In another bowl, whip the cream with the chocolate syrup until stiff. Add liqueur and beat to blend.

Combine beaten egg whites and whipped cream and beat together on low speed of your mixer until thoroughly combined.

Set 24 paper muffin cups in 2 muffin tins (12 each). Divide mixture between the 24 paper cups. Swirl 1 teaspoon of melted chocolate over each top. Place muffin tins in freezer and freeze until solid. Remove ice cream cups from the muffin tins and store in a box. Cover box with plastic wrap. Return to freezer.

When ready to serve, remove paper cup and place iced cream in a lovely stemmed glass or dessert dish. You can serve it plain or with a teaspoon of Creme de Cacao Liqueur spooned over the top. Or you may enjoy a dollup of whipped cream and some shaved chocolate. Makes 24 servings.

Chocolate Chip Chocolate Mousse

1/2 pound chocolate, sweet, broken into pieces
1 cup whipping cream
4 egg yolks
2 ounces chocolate, semi-sweet

Place chocolate pieces (can use chocolate chips) in blender container. Heat cream just to boiling point and pour into blender. Whip for about 1 minute. Add egg yolks and beat for another thirty seconds. Set mixture aside and allow to come to room temperature. Now add 2 ounces of chocolate and blend for about 20 or 30 seconds, or until chocolate is cut into little chips.

Pour mixture into 6 lovely stemmed glasses and place in refrigerator until firm. When you are ready to serve, spoon a teaspoon of Creme de Menthe or Creme de Cacao Liqueur over the chocolate. Decorate with a cherry or a dollup of whipped cream. Serves 6.

Note:
Please don't be misled by the simplicity of this delightful dessert. It is rich, so I kept the portions small.

This should be made a day ahead.

Remove from the refrigerator about 15 minutes before you are ready to serve.

Chocolate Mousse

1/2 pound chocolate, sweet or semi-sweet or some of each to taste
1 cup whipping cream
4 egg yolks

Place chocolate pieces in blender container. Heat cream to boiling point and pour into the blender. Blend for about 1 minute. Add egg yolks and beat for another 30 seconds. Divide mixture between 6 lovely stemmed glasses and refrigerate until firm. When ready to serve, spoon a teaspoon of Minted Chocolate or Cherry Chocolate Liqueur over the mousse. Serves 6.

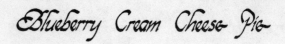

Blueberry Cream Cheese Pie

Very elegant, very lovely. This is one of my preferred pies.

1 1/4 cup graham cracker crumbs
1/2 cup chopped walnuts
1/3 cup butter, melted
3 tablespoons cinnamon sugar

Combine all the ingredients and mix until blended. Pat mixture on the bottom and sides of a buttered 9-inch pie pan. Bake in a 350° oven for about 8 minutes. Cool before filling.

CREAM AND CREAM CHEESE FILLING:

1 package (8 ounces) cream cheese
3/4 cup powdered sugar, sifted
1 teaspoon vanilla
1 teaspoon lemon zest
1 cup whipping cream

1 cup blueberry pie filling (canned)

Beat together the cream cheese, sugar and vanilla until the mixture is light and fluffy. Beat in the lemon zest.

In another bowl, beat the whipped cream until it is stiff. Fold together the cream and cream cheese mixture. (You can do this on the low setting of your electric mixer.) Pour Cream and Cream Cheese Filling into cooled pie shell, reserving about 3 tablespoons for decorating. Spread filling evenly and cover with blueberry pie filling. Decorate with little dollups of reserved cream mixture. Serves 8 with majesty.

Lemon Cloud Torte

MERINGUE SHELL:

4 egg whites
pinch of salt
pinch of cream of tartar
1 cup sugar

Beat egg whites until foamy. Add salt, cream of tartar and sugar, a little at a time, beating all the while until the meringue is stiff and glossy. Pour meringue into a heavily greased 9-inch pie pan and smooth it with a spatula. Bake in a 275° oven for 1 hour. Cool.

LEMON FILLING:

4 egg yolks
1/2 cup sugar
1/4 cup lemon juice, freshly squeezed
1 tablespoon finely grated lemon peel
1 pint whipping cream whipped with 2 tablespoons sugar

Beat egg yolks. On the top of a double boiler cook the egg yolks with the sugar, lemon juice and lemon peel. Cook and stir until mixture thickens. Allow to cool.

Add 1/2 of the whipped cream to the lemon mixture and fold it in. (Use the remaining cream to decorate the top of the pie. Pour filling into shell. Refrigerate overnight or for at least 6 hours. Before serving sprinkle with some finely grated lemon peel. Serves 6 to 8.

Nutcracker Pumpkin Pie

Don't think for a minute that these few simple ingredients will deliver a simple pumpkin pie. The pie is very different and the Galliano Whipped Cream topping is extravagant. Together they are totally delicious. This is a very unusual pumpkin pie.

3 egg whites
pinch of salt
pinch of cream of tartar
1 cup sugar

2/3 cup canned pumpkin
22 Ritz crackers, coarsley crumbled
1 1/2 teaspoons pumpkin pie spice (or to taste)

1 cup pecans (or walnuts), coarsely chopped
1 teaspoon vanilla

Beat egg whites until foamy. Add salt and cream of tartar and continue beating. Beat in sugar, 1/4 cup at a time, until egg whites are stiff and glossy. Add pumpkin and mix at low speed until blended. Add remaining ingredients and fold to combine. Pour mixture into a buttered 9-inch pie pan and bake in a preheated 350° oven for about 35-40 minutes. Top with Galliano Whipped Cream. Sprinkle with finely grated nuts. Serves 6 or 8.

Galliano Whipped Cream

1 cup heavy whipping cream
1 tablespoon sugar
1 tablespoon Galliano Liqueur

Beat chilled whipping cream with 1 tablespoon sugar until cream is thick. Add liqueur and beat until cream is stiff.

Note:
If you do not have Galliano on hand, you can substitute an orange flavored liqueur. The results will still be outstanding.

Puff paste in an instant?? No way . . . they say. And they are probably right. Puff pastry is one of the most majestic of doughs, but it's preparation is an arduous task that requires a great deal of time. Rolling, folding, turning, refrigerating, 6 times for Danish pastry, 8 times for the classic pastry, is a labor of much love and adoration. And it is well worth it too, if you happen to have the time.

However, if you do not, Quick Puff Paste is a little treasure that I hope you will enjoy. It is an amazingly simple dough, that is assembled in minutes and produces an incredibly delicate and flaky pastry very much like the regal puff paste. It handles so easily and requires so little attention that even the most inexperienced beginner will produce masterful results every time.

The number and combinations of fillings are inexhaustable. I have included, in the following, a few of my very favorites.

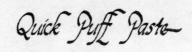

Quick Puff Paste

1 cup butter, salted
2 cups flour
1 cup sour cream

Cut butter into flour in your electric mixer until the mixture resembles coarse meal. (You can do this in your electric mixer with perfect results.) Add sour cream and beat for 30 seconds. Turn mixture out onto wax paper that is heavily dusted with flour. Sprinkle a little more flour over the dough for ease of handling. Shape into a ball and wrap in the floured wax paper. Refrigerate overnight. (Dough will keep for one week.)

To Assemble:
Divide dough into 4 parts. Working one part at a time, roll it out on a floured pastry cloth until dough measures about 10x10-inches. Spread 1/4 of the filling evenly over the dough. Roll jelly roll fashion ending with a strudel that measures 3x10-inches and seam side down.

Place strudel in a lightly greased pan. (Use a 12x16-inch pan so that you can bake the four strudels at one time.) Repeat with the remaining 3 parts of dough. Bake in a preheated 350° oven for about 30-35 minutes or until golden. Remove from the pan and cool. Sprinkle generously with sifted powdered sugar. Cut when cool.

Apricot Strudel with Walnuts

1 recipe Quick Puff Paste
1 cup apricot jam
1 cup chopped walnuts

Divide dough into 4 parts. Working one part at a time, roll it out on a floured pastry cloth until the dough measures about 10x10-inches. Spread 1/4 cup of apricot jam over the dough. Sprinkle with 1/4 cup of chopped walnuts. Roll jelly roll fashion ending with a strudel that measures 3x10-inches and is seam side down.

Place strudel on a lightly greased 12x16-inch pan. (You can bake the four strudels at one time.) Repeat with the remaining 3 parts of dough and filling.

Bake in a preheated 350° oven for about 30 minutes or until top is golden. Cool in the pan for 10 minutes and then cool strudels on a rack or a brown paper bag. Sprinkle generously with sifted powdered sugar. Cut when cool. Makes 24 to 30 slices.

Note:
Strudels can be frozen on a piece of cardboard and wrapped in plastic wrap and foil. Defrost uncovered. Do not freeze with the powdered sugar.

Chocolate Chip Danish

1 recipe Quick Puff Paste

12 tablespoons Nestle's Quik

1 package (6 ounces) milk chocolate chips or semi-sweet chocolate chips

Divide dough into 4 parts. Working one part at a time, roll it out on a floured pastry cloth until the dough measures about 10x10-inches. Spread 1/4 of the chocolate powder over the dough. Sprinkle with 1/4 of the chocolate chips. Roll jelly roll fashion ending with a roll that is about 3x10-inches and is seam side down.

Place Danish roll on a lightly greased 12x16-inch pan so that you can bake the four pastries at one time. Repeat with the remaining 3 parts of dough and filling.

Bake in a preheated 350° oven for about 30 minutes or until top is golden. Cool in the pan for 10 minutes. Remove from pan and continue cooling on a rack or a brown paper bag. Sprinkle generously with powdered sugar. Cut when cool. Makes 24-30 slices.

Note:
Danish can be frozen after they are baked. Place them uncut on a piece of cardboard and wrap them in plastic wrap and foil. Defrost them uncovered. Do not freeze them with the powdered sugar on top.

You are invited to join the
RECIPES-OF-THE-MONTH CLUB
Special gift rate saves you
$2 on every membership.

DONOR_____

Address_____

City_____ State_____ Zip_____

☐ Please include my membership at special rate.

☐ New   ☐ Renewal

☐ Send To_____

Address_____

City_____ State_____ Zip_____

☐ New   ☐ Renewal

Gift letter from _____

☐ Send To_____

Address_____

City_____ State_____ Zip_____

☐ New   ☐ Renewal

Gift letter from _____

☐ Additional membership orders enclosed

☐ I enclose $_____ for_____ memberships

Special Gift Rate
1 year membership $10
(Regular price $12)

**Recipes-of-the-Month Club
P.O. Box 5027
Beverly Hills, CA 90210**

Other cookbooks by Renny Darling
that you will LOVE and want to own . . .

☐ The Joy of Eating
  (8½ x 11 paper bound) $5.95*

☐ The Joy of Eating
  (8½ x 11 leather-like hard cover) $8.95*

☐ The Love of Eating
  (8½ x 11 paper bound) $5.95*

☐ The Love of Eating
  (8½ x 11 leather-like hard cover) $8.95*

☐ Renny Darling's Party Planner
  (8½ x 11 leather-like hard cover) $8.95*

☐ Selections from "The Joy of Eating"
  (4-3/8 x 7-1/4 paper bound) $2.25**

*Buy them at your local bookstore or use this handy
coupon for ordering.*

*Please add $1.00 postage and handling for each book.
**Please add $ .50 postage and handling for each book.
NO C.O.D.'s PLEASE

RECIPES-OF-THE-MONTH CLUB — DEPT AB
P.O. Box 5027 ● Beverly Hills, CA 90210

Please send me the books I have checked above. I am
enclosing $_____.

Mr./Mrs./Ms._____

Address_____

City_____ State_____ Zip_____

Please allow 4 weeks for delivery — Offer expires 12/78.
